STOP Probate NOW!

The Only Living Trust Book
You'll Ever Need

STOP
Probate
NOW!

The Only Living Trust Book You'll Ever Need

Warrick M. Graves
Joseph Leff

TRUST PUBLISHING COMPANY
10308 Metcalf, Suite 257
Overland Park, Kansas 66212
913-648-2712

FIRST EDITION

ISBN 0-9628529-0-2

Trust Publishing Company
Overland Park, Kansas 66212

Printed in the United States of America

DEDICATION

This book is dedicated to our wives, just for being there (even when we weren't), and especially for putting up with our work habits all these years; and to our children, who are the future; and to our parents and other relatives who always encouraged us to strive to be the best we could be.

ACKNOWLEDGMENTS

A book of this nature can succeed only with the cooperation of others. We'll take all the blame, though, for any errors, which of course are unintentional. Many thanks go to, alphabetically,

• Rita Clipp, Desktop Express, for her excellent typesetting ability and endless patience with our many corrections and amendments;

• Carla Garry, our hard-working Sales Assistant and overall Coordinator, for assisting us in so many important ways too numerous to list;

• J. Ransdell Keene; Keene, Auer & Antee; for sharing his estate planning and extensive Trust experience and legal insight;

• Robert Labine, PHFF, for sharing his knowledge and expertise in estate planning developed over decades;

• Courtney Smith, Independence Trust Company, for his outstanding estate planning advice and his willingness to share his many years of experience unstintingly;

• William Steinhardt, Steinhardt Direct, for his strategic planning skills and ability to share his extensive experience with us;

• James H. Thompson, Jr., Thompson & Danaher, for his superb legal advice and his wise counsel;

• Bruce Tolbert, The House of Trust, for his technical advice and for sharing his many insights with the public; and

• Peggy Wink, Graphic Specialties, for her artwork (and that of her capable staff) and for outstanding design work and assistance.

Introduction

The contents of this book have been prepared to provide a comprehensive view of the benefits and structure of The Revocable Living Trust as they relate to the escalating expenses of Probating an estate and the measures that can be recommended to avoid Probate. The material presented will help the reader communicate more meaningfully with qualified professionals in the legal, para-legal, tax, Trust processing and estate planning fields.

Neither the publisher nor the authors imply that this book serves as a substitute for such qualified specialists as mentioned above. Instead, they encourage individuals of all economic levels who have Life Insurance, retirement benefits, disability coverage, home ownership and other assets to use the knowledge learned in this book to maximize their conferences with the proper professional counselor for the preparation of a specifically designed Trust document.

As stockbrokers and financial advisers with New York Stock Exchange member firms, we noticed this pattern during the last several years: some of our clients were passing on. Of those who did, the great majority had their estates go through the costs and delays of Probate. But we observed that some estates avoided Probate, thereby enabling the heirs to participate in a smoother, less expensive, transition.

In *every* instance of a smoother inheritance by the Beneficiaries of an estate, the instrument easing the way was a **Revocable Living Trust**. In most Probated situations, the deceased had a Will. In the rest, the deceased had done nothing, thereby dying *intestate*, or without a Will, allowing the state to distribute their estate to their heirs, subject to rigid state statute.

When our clients' estates went through Probate, *we*, as their financial advisers, went through Probate with them. Probate is a nonproductive waste of valuable time, especially since it can be avoided through proper planning. And the duration of many Probate situations seems interminable.

Because we firmly believe that our clients' interests come first, we recommended to them the **Revocable Living Trust**. Through all our years of working with attorneys, counseling estate planning specialists, attending seminars, conducting workshops, reading books and evaluating other publications, the evidence reinforced our advice about the **Revocable Living Trust**. It is far superior to a Will. Indeed, you could call it a "super will" or a "private will."

There are three compelling points you must keep in mind these days.

1. If you have people you care about and love—such as a spouse, children, grandchildren, other family members, friends or even charities—you need a **Revocable Living Trust**.

2. If you are concerned about incapacity making you unable to manage your financial affairs, you need a **Revocable Living Trust**.

3. If you are concerned about Federal Estate Taxes reducing the assets available to your heirs, you need a **Revocable Living Trust**.

The longer we continued to develop seminars for our clients and the general public, the more we felt as though we were on a crusade. Truly it has grown into an ardent, impassioned campaign to inform the public about the pros and cons of avoiding Probate by using one of the oldest techniques around, the **Revocable Living Trust**. At the same time, it has been our intent to expose the myths of and demystify the enigma of this useful vehicle. These are key steps to effective estate planning.

You may rightfully ask how you know if you need a **Revocable Living Trust.** The answer is simple. If you own something of value that you want somebody or some charity to receive *100 percent* of, then you need a **Revocable Living Trust**.

How complicated, how expensive is it? Read on.

What follows is an explanation in plain English, using a minimum of technical terms. There's a Glossary at the end which you may find useful.

TABLE OF CONTENTS

Chapter 1
Myths of the Will

"When There's A Will There's A Way."
—Old Saying

"I have a Will, so I know my family and I are well-protected." Estate Planners and attorneys hear this frequently. You may be surprised to learn that this statement is not accurate. In fact, it has several inaccuracies in it, explicit and implied.

The person who believes he or she is protected by a Will could not be more mistaken. After all, a Will is activated after someone dies; it doesn't do anything for the person while he or she lives.

Following are eight circumstances where the Will does not have you well-protected.

1. DISABILITY

Insurance industry statistics indicate that you may be among the majority of people who will suffer at least one long-term disability before death. Whether that disability is caused by illness, by accident or by old age, a Will serves absolutely no purpose. If you become incapacitated and cannot handle your affairs, your estate may go through a Conservatorship, thereby involving the Probate Court. A Will is for after you die.

The person who repeats the statement in the first line of this chapter may go through life comfortably believing his family is being protected. The truth is much less comforting.

You see, leaving your assets to your loved ones by

means of a Will is like using a cracked pipeline to deliver gas to your house or water to your garden. Some gas or water gets there and some doesn't. In fact, it's possible for the Probate system to be the largest single Beneficiary of your estate because up to 15 percent or more of your estate can be used to cover legal fees, court costs and other administrative fees. Is that your intent?

2. DELAYS

Furthermore, if your family "is being well-protected" by means of a Will, the implication is that this happens on a timely basis. This also is not true. It's unusual for a Will to be Probated in less than six months; it can take years. For example, John Wayne died in 1979. As of December 1989, his estate was still in Probate. And the costs continued to escalate, further reducing the amount of actual dollars that will get into the hands of his heirs.

And the delays are plentiful. An estate which is delayed costs more to clear. It costs more in dollars, in energy, in frustration and in lost opportunity. Anything which causes a delay raises the cost of Probate, thereby reducing the benefits your heirs receive.

If real estate or other assets are held in more than one state, then multiple-probate situations would occur, causing even more delays. In other words, each state will have jurisdiction over the property located in that state.

3. PROBATE

Some people believe a Will avoids Probate. Wrong. A Will *must* go through Probate. In fact, Probate is defined as the process of legally validating a Will.

4. MINORS

If your Will leaves something to minor children or grandchildren, are you aware they can't get it? At least, they cannot own such assets directly while they are minors. Many of the state laws typically show 18-21 as the age of majority. Many Wills provide for Guardians for minors, but few provide for Custodians for their assets. Guardians and Custodians do not have to be the same people. If a Custodian is not appointed, the Probate Court will do so—for a fee. And your Will can only recommend a Guardian; the Probate Court makes the final decision as to this appointment.

5. PUBLICITY

Another common expression is, "Well, at least after I'm gone, my family can go on about it's own private business, thanks to my Will."

This is another misconception. A Will, because of the Probate process, is open to public scrutiny. As your Will enters Probate, it and a *complete inventory* of your assets are put on file—available to the public—in the Probate Division of your county courthouse. This information is available just for the asking. *Anyone* has the right to examine your file. This means friends, nosey neighbors and Probate opportunists—including those standing in line to make a few dollars from your estate.

In fact, an estate which is "Probated" by a Will must *advertise* that the person has died. Your local newspaper likely runs such ads regularly.

6. CHALLENGE

It's easy to challenge, or contest, the terms of a Will. The advertisements previously mentioned encourage a challenge from a disgruntled relative or friend.

Sometimes the purpose of such a challenge is not to win, but to be compensated for not causing additional delays.

7. COSTS

What are the costs in dollars? Probate costs typically include:

1. Probate Court fees
2. Attorney fees
3. Publicity fees
4. Appraisal fees
5. Auctioneer fees
6. Accountant fees
7. Secured debts
8. Administrative fees
9. Miscellaneous Probate fees
10. Extraordinary fees

All of the above costs can be avoided completely.

They are unnecessary. Recent studies indicate that these costs average about 4 percent to 10 percent of the *gross value* of an estate. For example, if your house is worth $100,000 with a $40,000 mortgage balance remaining, the fee will be assessed on the $100,000 gross value. After all costs are paid, the Probate Court distributes what is left to the Beneficiaries.

On smaller estates (those under $100,000), the cost in percentage terms is higher. Surveys show that Probate costs sometimes run more than 20 percent.

Obviously, all the above reduce what is left to the heirs or Beneficiaries of the estate. So who gains by means of Probate?

There are those who argue that Probate is necessary in order to protect the claims of creditors. Generally, there is a small number of bills (fewer than a dozen) filed with the Probate Court, and usually they are small relative to the size of the estate. Many people have medical insurance which covers a sizable portion of medical bills.

Usually the creditor pays fees and is involved with other paperwork in filing claims with Probate Court. Remember, your heirs are responsible for your bills only up to the amount they inherit.

So who does benefit from Probate? You will find it interesting to examine the following sequence for paying claims against the estate.

In most states, attorneys' fees come first, even before taxes. It doesn't matter if there are sufficient assets to pay creditors, or to leave assets to heirs. The attorneys in those cases get paid first.

A very small estate may avoid Probate. For example, the Kansas Bar Association says that "when the deceased leaves a spouse or minor children...a simplified proceeding referred to as Refusal to Grant Letters of Administration may be used."

This process is similar in many states and explains how a very small estate avoids Probate.

8. CONSERVATORSHIP

It's possible to find your estate in Probate while you're alive—which could result in an estate being Probated more than once.

Remember, a Will does not address disability. If you're

disabled to the point of severe incapacity, and your signature is needed on a document, how can your signature be obtained?

A Conservatorship, or Guardianship, would be established—typically under the supervision of the Probate Court—to do so. If you own real estate or securities jointly, for example, in order for it to be sold, all joint owners' signatures are needed.

These eight examples certainly are convincing reasons why a Will is not the way to prevent many problems. It's certainly *not* the way to avoid Probate.

INTESTATE (NO WILL)

Some people leave no written instructions whatsoever. This is referred to as dying *Intestate*. State law would then distribute assets according to a legal formula which varies by state—after going through Probate. A Will is better than nothing since at least your intentions are in writing.

Chapter 2
Myths of Joint Ownership

"With this ring I thee wed, with my body I thee worship, and with all my worldly goods I thee endow."

—**Book of Common Prayer**

Because most married couples own most of their assets in joint ownership, you should understand the myths of joint ownership. Many assets also are held jointly by parents and children, often in an ineffective attempt to avoid Probate and expedite inheritance.

The most frequently used form of joint ownership is Joint Tenants With Right of Survivorship, commonly abbreviated as JTWROS or Jt. Ten. Other forms of joint ownership include Tenancy By The Entirety, and Tenants In Common. All these are described below.

JOINT TENANTS WITH RIGHT OF SURVIVORSHIP

You don't have to be married or even related to use this form of ownership. This form is widely used and understood. Although it implies *"and"* so that each person must be involved in transacting business, most financial institutions build in powers-of-attorney on signature forms. The powers-of-attorney effectively permit any participant to act. Jointly-held real estate, however, is "pure" joint ownership. It requires the signatures of *all* participants to be sold. This also is true for securities transactions.

TENANCY BY THE ENTIRETY

Tenancy By The Entirety is not valid in all 50 states. It is available only to husband and wife, usually for real estate. Its biggest advantage is that this form of ownership makes it very difficult for a creditor to attach real estate. The form is especially valuable in protecting the ownership of a married couple's residence. The death of one spouse allows the surviving spouse to inherit without Probate.

A divorce of the couple owning assets in Tenancy By The Entirety will automatically change the title to Tenants in Common.

TENANTS IN COMMON

Tenants In Common means that there is *no right of survivorship.* The deceased party's share is passed according to his or her Will, or by state laws in the absence of a Will, to the deceased's descendants. This method of ownership also does *not* avoid Probate.

MORE ON JTWROS

In a technical sense, Joint Tenants With Right of Survivorship (JTWROS) *does* avoid Probate—as long as there is at least one survivor. Effectively, Probate is *deferred,* not avoided. It is deferred only until the last survivor dies.

Furthermore, JTWROS is simple to understand and implement. It is familiar to the clerks at the financial institutions, as well as to stockbrokers, insurance agents and real estate agents. The whole financial industry has been trained to recommend the JTWROS form of titling assets because of its simplicity. The question is this: *Is it best for you?*

If one party is incapacitated, JTWROS permits the other(s) to act, as long as *"or"* appears in the title or if there is a Durable Power of Attorney involved. These are all very useful positive aspects of JTWROS. The case of Alice and Bill Carpenter follows.

Alice and Bill have been married for several years. They carefully titled their savings and checking accounts and residence as:

Alice Carpenter and Bill Carpenter JTWROS

Signature cards at the bank also included a power of attorney, effectively changing the account to *"or."*

Bill dies. The estate does *not* go through Probate—for now. Remember—JTWROS *defers* Probate; it doesn't avoid it. (See Figure 1.)

Although Alice still can write checks against the joint account, she should change the title on all accounts. She'll also need an "original" death certificate for each account, as well as additional documentation which is required by each state. This requirement varies somewhat from state to state.

Alice *cannot* sell the house without retitling the house into her name only. That's because real estate requires *all* signatures. If Alice wants to sell the house without retitling it, she'll need to go to court, usually Probate Court, to do so.

However, if Bill doesn't die, but instead is severely incapacitated, Alice still can write checks against the joint account. Strictly speaking, she *cannot* transact business in their securities account, although many stockbrokers may not be completely familiar with these rules. This creates the possibility of litigation, especially if Bill recovers and

FIGURE 1

BILL AND ALICE, JTWROS

BILL HAS DIED,

LEAVING ALICE,
WHO OWNS THE ASSETS.

PROBATE IS DELAYED.

disagrees with what was done during his incapacity.

The biggest problem, however, arises with real estate because the signatures of *all* parties are required to consummate a sale. Although Bill is incapacitated and can't sign his own name, somebody must sign for him. This is accomplished by a court, usually Probate Court, establishing a *Conservatorship* or *Guardianship* for Bill. In some jurisdictions, however, it is a Magistrate's Court which performs this function. A *Conservator* or *Guardian* is appointed by the judge. This is frequently an attorney, who gets paid to perform this function. (See Figure 2.)

Bill and Alice are back in Probate again.

Establishing such a Conservatorship takes time as well as money. The delays of Conservatorship could cause Alice to miss an opportunity to sell a property on a timely basis. Many other activities can be slowed down. And if Alice dies, leaving Bill incapacitated, *all* decisions would then be made by the Conservator for the duration of Bill's incapacity.

All this can be avoided by means of a Revocable Living Trust and associated documents. There are additional myths of joint tenancy.

The family of Dave and Ellen Farrell includes three children: George, Harriet and Irene. Dave is 63, Ellen is 61, and their children are 40, 38 and 36 respectively.

Dave and Ellen are concerned about distributing assets to their children after their own deaths. Their oldest child and only son, George, lives nearby with his wife, Janet. Harriet and Irene are also married, but live in different parts of the country. Dave and Ellen are aware that Joint Tenancy is a means of providing for the survivor(s) to own property after the death of one or more joint owners. George is a dutiful son and has excellent relations with his sisters. So they put George down as joint

FIGURE 2

BILL AND ALICE, JTWROS
BILL IS DISABLED.
ALICE IS NOT.
TO SELL REAL ESTATE, BOTH SIGNATURES ARE REQUIRED.
JUDGE
SO A CONSERVATORSHIP IS ESTABLISHED IN ORDER TO ACCOMPLISH THIS.

owner, with them, on their assets with the understanding by all that, after Dave and Ellen are gone, George will share the assets equally with his two sisters. Dave and Ellen are confident in George and know he'll follow this arrangement.

Now, property reads:

Dave Farrell and
Ellen Farrell and
George Farrell JTWROS

A few months later, Dave and Ellen die together in a common occurrence accident. George now owns everything outright. Several scenarios emerge just after the death of George's parents.

Case 1: George dies shortly after his parents do before he is able to retitle or distribute the assets. As for Harriet and Irene, they just got disinherited. George's widow, Janet, *may* get it all. This is an example of "Murphy's Law" at work. (See Figure 3)

Case 2: George doesn't die. In fact, while his folks are still alive, George is in an auto accident and gets sued. Now a new danger arises: Mom and Dad's property can be attached! Even if George's wife, Janet, who has grown hostile, sues for divorce, she also can tie up the property. (See Figure 4.)

Case 3: Worried about the possibility of George's death disinheriting Harriet and Irene, Dave and Ellen decide to put all their children's names on their property, so that the title now reads:

Dave Farrell and
Ellen Farrell and
George Farrell and
Harriet Farrell and
Irene Farrell JTWROS

FIGURE 3

CASE 1

DAVE FARRELL AND
ELLEN FARRELL AND
GEORGE FARRELL, JTWROS

DAVE AND ELLEN
DIE TOGETHER.

GEORGE INHERITS,
BUT DIES BEFORE BEING
ABLE TO ARRANGE TO
RETITLE OR REDISTRIBUTE
ASSETS.

GEORGE'S WIFE, JANET, MAY GET
IT ALL, DISINHERITING GEORGE'S
SISTERS, HARRIET AND IRENE.

FIGURE 4

CASE 2

DAVE FARRELL AND
ELLEN FARRELL AND
GEORGE FARRELL, JTWROS

GEORGE IS IN AN ACCIDENT.

WITH GEORGE'S NAME ON PROPERTY, THAT PROPERTY CAN BE ATTACHED, OR THREATENED TO BE ATTACHED.

Again, on the death of one or more, the remaining survivors own the assets without going through Probate...for now. This is a case where the cure may be worse than the disease. Here's how. (See Figure 5.)

Case 4: Let's say that Dave and Ellen now want to sell their home. Having just retired, they want to move to a nice, warm climate and will use the proceeds of the home sale to purchase their retirement home. However, there are some problems with this.

First, they need everyone's signature on all the real estate sale documents. In addition, in many states *they'll need signatures of their children's spouses*. This can be so *even if the children got married after their names got put on the deed!* (See Figure 6.)

George's sisters, Harriet and Irene, continue to use their maiden names even though they're both married. It makes it easier to identify them.

But George's widow, Janet, who always had been hostile, could hold up the whole process because she's feeling out of sorts.

On the other hand, if everyone is in a cooperative mood and all documents receive all the appropriate signatures in a timely manner, this will be *very costly* to Dave and Ellen.

That's because there's a once-in-a-lifetime special income tax exemption on the profit on up $125,000 on the sale of a residence. It's for anyone over age 55 who's lived in the residence for at least three out of the past five years. Dave and Ellen are both over age 55, so they qualify. They do qualify, except...George, Harriet and Irene are each under age 55. Good-by to the majority of this exemption, which is prorated, instead of 100 percent. The IRS will receive a larger tax payment due to this oversight. (See Figure 7.)

FIGURE 5

IF ONE OR MORE DIES, THE SURVIVORS OWN THE ASSETS WITHOUT GOING THROUGH PROBATE... FOR NOW.

YES, GEORGE'S SISTERS, HARRIET AND IRENE, CONTINUE TO USE THEIR MAIDEN NAMES, EVEN THOUGH THEY'RE BOTH MARRIED. IT CERTAINLY MAKES IT EASIER FOR US TO IDENTIFY THEM.

FIGURE 6

CASE 4

DAVE AND ELLEN WANT TO SELL THE HOUSE. NOT ONLY ARE ALL FIVE SIGNATURES REQUIRED, BUT THEY MAY NEED ALL SPOUSES' SIGNATURES AS WELL.

- DAVE AND ELLEN FARRELL ☑
- GEORGE AND JANET FARRELL ☑
- HARRIET FARRELL AND HUSBAND ☑
- IRENE FARRELL AND HUSBAND ☑

FIGURE 7

MORE CASE 4

THEY OBTAINED ALL EIGHT SIGNATURES LISTED IN FIGURE 6, AND WERE HAPPY TO GET A GOOD PRICE FOR SELLING THE HOUSE.

THEY ESTABLISHED A GAIN OF $125,000 ON THE SALE PRICE OF THEIR HOUSE. THAT'S WHEN THEY SPOKE TO THEIR ACCOUNTANT, WHO POINTED OUT THE FORFEIT OF MOST OF THEIR OVER-55 EXEMPTION. THIS GAIN BECAME MOSTLY TAXABLE.

Case 5: All five names appear on the home, as in cases 3 and 4. In this case, Dave and Ellen die. Their three children inherit the home, *without* going through Probate.

When you inherit from a deceased person, you inherit at the "stepped-up" basis in value. This is the fair market value of assets as of the date of death, or as of six months later, whichever is more to the advantage of the heirs. Having George, Harriet and Irene on the deed will negate this to a great extent. After all, they had partial ownership before Dave and Ellen died. Consequently, they will forfeit the portion of the gain that represents their pro rata share of the step-up in basis—60 percent, or 3/5. That's expensive! (See Figure 8.)

Furthermore, there may be gift tax complications, too, dating to the time the names were added to the deed or other assets.

Before adding someone else's name to your property, you should *carefully* review potential complications with your tax adviser.

Better still, implement a Revocable Living Trust and avoid those complications completely.

Although there are other potential complications of Joint Tenancy With Right of Survivorship, the situations discussed in this chapter are enough to expose some of the Myths of Joint Ownership.

FIGURE 8

CASE 5

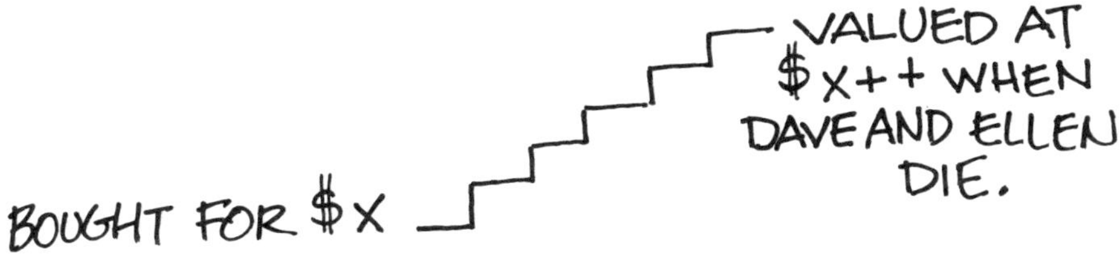

THE "STEPPED-UP" BASIS IS SUBSTANTIALLY FORFEITED, AND IT WASN'T NECESSARY TO DO SO!

Chapter 3
Myths of Trusts

"Who Do You Trust?"
—TV Game Show, starring Johnny Carson

"In God We Trust."
—American Currency

In the literature on Trusts and in seminars on estate planning, many statements have been made and questions raised to demonstrate how widespread are the publicly-held Myths of Trusts. Five of the most common Myths are described below.

MYTH #1: TRUSTS ARE ONLY FOR THE RICH.

Court records show that estates from small sizes to huge amounts go through Probate. The Probate process sometimes takes a year or more, and is expensive. Ask anyone who's experienced Probate how annoying it is. Most states have a minimum size estate for Probate. That minimum may be as low as $20,000. Since Revocable Living Trusts avoid Probate, they *can* be used by people of modest means.

MYTH #2: TRUSTS ARE VERY EXPENSIVE.

In a survey of several markets across the country, the cost of a Revocable Living Trust averaged around $1100. Several cities reflected both higher minimums and higher maximums. A Revocable Living Trust need not be priced outrageously high.

MYTH #3: ESTABLISHING A REVOCABLE LIVING TRUST REQUIRES TIME—ESPECIALLY COSTLY ATTORNEY'S TIME.

Certainly it can be done this way, but it isn't required. Just as it isn't necessary to go through Probate, it isn't necessary to use enormous amounts of costly attorney's time to establish a Revocable Living Trust. Less than 10 percent of the 600,000-plus attorneys know how to prepare Revocable Living Trusts. Trust publishing and processing firms can provide you with inexpensive Revocable Living Trusts, allowing you a less costly means of avoiding Probate. Trusts need not be very expensive.

MYTH #4: JOINT OWNERSHIP WILL KEEP ME OUT OF PROBATE. I DON'T NEED THE TRUST. IN FACT, JUST TO BE SAFE, LET'S PUT OUR ADULT CHILD'S NAME ON OUR ASSETS.

The many pitfalls of joint ownership were discussed in Chapter 2. *At best,* joint ownership will delay Probate. It won't avoid it.

MYTH #5: A TRUST MUST BE ADMINISTERED BY A BANK TRUST COMPANY.

This is one of the most widely-held misconceptions. Most Revocable Living Trusts are managed by the same people who administer their own lives, just as they always have. Backup or "Successor" Trustees are usually the same people you would have appointed as Executors of your Will—your children, other family members, friends. Certainly a trust department or trust company can do that for you, but the great majority of people prefer not to use that costly method.

You *can* avoid administrative costs if you want to. The point is that use of a trust company is not necessary. Then again, strictly speaking, Probate is unnecessary, too. You can leave your estate to your loved ones or to the Probate process. You have a choice.

Don't fall prey to these Myths, because that could cost your family thousands of dollars unnecessarily. If you can answer Yes to these three questions, you should protect your heirs with a Revocable Living Trust.

1. Do you have anything worth saving?
2. Do you want to save it?
3. Do you have someone for whom to save it?

Chapter 4
What Is a Revocable Living Trust?

"Absence makes the heart grow fonder."
—Thomas H. Bayly, *Isle of Beauty*

"Accidents will occur in the best-regulated families."
—Charles Dickens, *David Copperfield*

"All I know is what I read in the papers."
—Will Rogers

There have been numerous newspaper and magazine articles on the Revocable Living Trust in the last few years. While only recently getting public attention, the Revocable Living Trust has been around for a long time. It first became popular during the Middle Ages, especially for European nobility who went off to fight in the Crusades. A noble who did so had to "trust" someone to take care of his estate for him, while the noble was still alive. Even Lady Godiva was covered by a Living Trust—and not by much else on her famous ride!

While there are more than 40 types of Trusts in use today, they share some common definitions.

SOME DEFINITIONS

A **Trust** is a legal contract or agreement whereby one or more persons or institutions controls property owned by another person or persons for the benefit of one or more third parties.

The person(s) giving the property are called the *Grantor(s)* or *Trustor(s)* or *Settlor(s)* or *Donor(s)* or

Creator(s).

The person controlling the property is called the *Trustee.*

The person who benefits from the Trust is called the *Beneficiary.*

Two frequently used types of Trusts are the Testamentary Trust and the Revocable Living Trust.

TESTAMENTARY TRUST

The **Testamentary Trust** typically is associated with a Will. A Testamentary Trust takes effect after death and *after Probate.* A Testamentary Trust will be terminated, or dissolved, after all assets within it have been distributed to the named Beneficiaries in accordance with Trust terms.

There are several major disadvantages to the Testamentary Trust. They include the following:

1. Probate is *not* avoided.
2. Disability is *not* addressed.
3. Estate taxes may n*ot* be reduced.
4. Strictly speaking, a Testamentary Trust is *not* always necessary. After all, the Will with which it is associated provides for asset distribution, after death and after Probate.

REVOCABLE LIVING TRUST

Much more desirable than the Testamentary Trust is the Revocable Living Trust, which you establish while you are alive. The Revocable Living Trust is terminated after the distribution of all assets to the named Beneficiaries in accordance with Trust terms. The Revocable Living Trust *avoids* the costs, delays and seemingly interminable hassles of Probate. This is the key reason for it's use.

The second most important reason is that a Revocable Living Trust, with associated documents, will allow for the orderly continuation of your financial and business affairs should you be disabled or incapacitated because of an accident, illness or age. Thus, you will *not* be placed into a court-ordered Conservatorship or Guardianship if you cannot manage your own affairs.

Estate taxes ca*n* be reduced or even eliminated by using a Revocable Living Trust.

And the Revocable Living Trust does become necessary for the timely and orderly distribution of your assets after you're gone according to your wishes as expressed in your Revocable Living Trust.

REVOCABLE LIVING TRUST PUTS YOU IN CONTROL

Many people, when considering the Revocable Living Trust, express concerns about *giving up control* of their assets to a Trustee. In fact, a Revocable Living Trust actually *increases* their control over their assets while they're alive and *even after their demise*. It does so because they can occupy all three positions held by people in a Revocable Living Trust—*Grantor, Trustee* and *Beneficiary*. These positions are described below, and show how they can work for you.

1. **GRANTOR**

The Grantor establishes the Revocable Living Trust, granting the ability for it to exist by transferring title of assets to the Trustee of the Trust. This process is called *"Retitling."*

2. **TRUSTEE**

You as Trustee control, or manage, the Trust assets.

Because *you can be the Trustee*, in effect you can give *yourself* (husbands and wives can give *themselves*) control of property you own. If you're managing your affairs now, *without* a Trust, you can continue to do so *with* a Revocable Living Trust. As Trustee, you can continue to buy, sell, invest, borrow, lease, rent and so forth, just as you do now. If you desire, you can give assets away.

John D. Rockefeller is reputed to have said, "I don't want to own things. I just want to control things." The Revocable Living Trust enables you to do this.

3. BENEFICIARY

Of course, Trust activity is to be for the benefit of the Beneficiary, you. While you're alive, *you* can be Grantor, Trustee and Beneficiary of your Trust. Of course, you will name one or more Beneficiaries to receive assets after you die. But at the outset the Beneficiary, to repeat, is *you*.

Every asset retitled to the Trust belongs to the Trust and escapes Probate. It's important to the successful use of the Trust that you retitle your assets. Those assets that are left out of the Trust can be Probated. If you retitle nothing, it means you haven't established your Trust—and you'd be wasting your time. Unfortunately, there are many examples where professionals encounter case after case where a Revocable Living Trust was established, but assets were not retitled. That left assets unprotected. This is like buying a new car, but not putting in fuel.

There is even the case of a prominent doctor who suddenly learned that he had had an empty Trust for over five years. He immediately saved his family tens of thousands of dollars, as he began retitling his assets that same afternoon. His attorney evidently had not informed him of the importance of retitling. Attorneys are not the only ones capable of properly advising you about your Trust. Many qualified Estate Planners can assist you in this matter, too. Remember, less than 10 percent of attorneys know how to prepare a Revocable Living Trust.

Below is an example of how a Revocable Living Trust develops.

Remember the Farrell family in Chapter 2? They tried to use Joint Tenancy to avoid Probate and created more problems than they solved. Here's how they solved these problems using the Revocable Living Trust for assets that fall within the $600,000 Federal Estate Tax exemption.

Dave Farrell and Ellen Farrell, husband and wife, establish a Revocable Living Trust. They are Grantors, Trustees and Beneficiaries. After they're both deceased, they want their assets distributed equally to their three children, George, Harriet and Irene. They want to avoid all forms of Probate and Conservatorships.

Because Dave and Ellen Farrell are joint Trustees, on the death of one spouse, the survivor will retain control of the Trust, continuing to receive income from assets and retaining the ability to buy and sell assets, as before.

SUCCESSOR TRUSTEES

When they set up the Revocable Living Trust, Dave and Ellen made provisions for Successor Trustees to back them up. Their oldest child, son George, always exhibited a great deal of common sense and good judgment. This was so, even though his wife, Janet, is hostile. So Dave and Ellen, with George's acceptance, made George the **Successor Trustee.** It is George's job to step in for Dave and Ellen if *neither* can function because of death, disability or both.

George can do so only with two physicians' signed statements about incompetence while either Dave or Ellen still lives. George will distribute assets after both parents' demise, according to Trust terms.

Unlike Executors in some states, none of the Trustees, Successor Trustees, or Contingent Successor Trustees are required to live in the same state as the Grantor(s).

CONTINGENT SUCCESSOR TRUSTEE

Dave and Ellen wanted to allow for a backup for George—"just in case." Harriet, the second oldest child and older of the two daughters, is not good at handling money and generally exercises poor judgment. Her husband is not good with money either, and Dave and Ellen fear he might influence Harriet negatively.

Because the parents recognized that establishing a Revocable Living Trust is not a popularity contest, they decided to appoint their youngest child, Irene, as **Contingent Successor Trustee**, to be a backup to George. Irene's husband would likely not interfere; he has no head for finances and defers to Irene in such matters. Furthermore, he has no legal right to do so.

So the Dave and Ellen Farrell Trust has filled all positions (See Figure 9):

1. Grantors - Dave and Ellen Farrell
2. Trustees - Dave and Ellen Farrell

2a. Successor Trustees - George Farrell, son

2b. Contingent Successor Trustee - Irene Farrell, daughter

3. Beneficiaries - Dave and Ellen Farrell

3a. Beneficiaries after death—children to share equally.

Incidentally, Dave and Ellen can hold all three positions only if at least one Successor Trustee is named.

Because this is a Revocable Living Trust, Dave and Ellen have the right to change or completely cancel the Trust. Most amendments involve changes in Beneficiary

FIGURE 9

THE DAVE AND ELLEN FARRELL REVOCABLE LIVING TRUST.

DAVE AND ELLEN FARRELL

GEORGE FARRELL (SON) IS SUCCESSOR TRUSTEE.

IRENE FARRELL (DAUGHTER) IS CONTINGENT SUCCESSOR TRUSTEE.

HARRIET
GEORGE IRENE

ARE TO SHARE ASSETS EQUALLY, AFTER BOTH PARENTS ARE GONE.

or Successor Trustee.

Changes of Beneficiary seem to occur most often due to the birth of a new grandchild or the death of a named Beneficiary.

Changes of Successor Trustee seem to occur with the death or incapacity of a Successor Trustee or when one moves to a distant location.

Chapter 5
How a Revocable Living Trust Can Reduce Federal Estate Taxes

"In this world nothing is certain but death and taxes."
—Benjamin Franklin, Letter (in French) to Leroy, 1789.

"Taxation without representation is tyranny."
—James Otis, *Argument on... Writs of Assistance* (1769)

"For dust thou art, and until dust shalt thou return."
—Old Testament, *Genesis, III,* 19

The Federal government taxes some estates when the owners die. Currently the first $600,000 is exempt. If there were no exemption, the first $600,000 of an estate would be taxed in the amount of $192,800. Please note that there is an *unlimited marital exemption,* so if one spouse dies, no Federal Estate Taxes are due until the second spouse dies.

If an estate is valued below $600,000, there is no Federal Estate Tax charge. When the figure exceeds $600,000, some estate tax planning becomes necessary. Federal Estate Taxes are expensive! (See Figure 10 for a chart.) The 1981 tax law *raised* the exemption in steps to $600,000. In 1981, it was less than $176,000. Only about 3 percent of estates exceed $600,000. A bill has been introduced recently in the U.S. Congress to reduce this exemption to $225,000. This means many more estates would be taxed because of the exemption rollback.

Sometimes estate taxes and inheritance taxes are referred to as "Death Taxes."

Figure 10.

Estate Tax Chart

Estate Size	Tax *	Plus % of Excess
$ 600,000	$ 192,800	37%
$ 750,000	$ 248,300	39%
$ 1,000,000	$ 345,800	41%
$ 1,500,000	$ 555,800	45%
$ 2,000,000	$ 780,800	49%
$ 2,500,000	$ 1,025,800	53%
$ 3,000,000	$ 1,290,800	55%
$ 5,000,000	$ 2,390,800	55%
$ 7,500,000	$ 3,765,800	55%
$10,000,000	$ 5,140,800	55%
$15,000,000	$ 7,890,800	55%
$20,000,000	$10,640,800	55%

*Subtract $192,800 to allow for the $600,000 exemption. These figures include a *5 percent surtax* on estates between $10,000,000 and $21,040,000.

There are three important concepts about Federal Estate Taxes:

1. They *MUST* be paid.
2. They must be paid in *CASH.*
3. They must be paid in cash *WITHIN NINE MONTHS OF DEATH.*

About half the United States (and Washington, D.C.) have inheritance taxes, too. Because the list changes from time to time, you should contact your local taxing authority to determine the status of your estate.

Various surveys show that most people significantly underestimate the value of their estates. As an exercise, estimate yours now. Then add up the pieces, one by one, and compare the two figures.

There's an important difference in the way Probate fees and Federal Estate Taxes are calculated. The former are against *Gross Estates*, while the latter are on *Net Estates* (after deducting all liabilities and debts).

Calculating an estate typically includes the following:

Home
Autos
Personal Property
Investments (CDs, stocks, bonds, annuities, etc.)
Life Insurance (Face value, or insurance amount not cash value.)
Retirement Plans

For some reason, Life Insurance is omitted by the public about half the time. Whether you include all your assets or not, the IRS will. And if your estate exceeds $1 million, owning Life Insurance directly may not be the best strategy. In other words, if your estate exceeds $1 million *excluding* Life Insurance, your Life Insurance should not be included in your estate. See the discussion in the next chapter.

The asset most frequently omitted by the general public is retirement plans. This includes Pension, Profit-Sharing, Section 403(b) Tax-Sheltered Annuities, 401(k) Plans, IRAs, IRA Rollovers, Keoghs and Employee Stock Ownership Plans (ESOPs). For some this category of asset represents a very significant total.

ONE EXEMPTION OR TWO

It's apparent that two unrelated persons will qualify for two $600,000 exemptions. Although it therefore would be natural to assume that a husband and wife likewise would qualify for these two exemptions, totalling $1.2 million, this is not the case.

If a husband and wife own property in Joint Tenancy as most husbands and wives do, then they qualify for only one exemption.

If a husband and wife own assets, some in his name and some in hers—with the surviving spouse to inherit the deceased spouse's assets—then they qualify for only *one* exemption.

THE REVOCABLE LIVING TRUST TO THE RESCUE

If neither joint ownership nor separate ownership works, a married couple can turn to the Revocable Living Trust.

However, what is involved here is a special form of the Revocable Living Trust. Some call it the "A-B Trust," some the "His-and-Hers Trust;" there are other names as well. The "His-and-Hers Trust" seems to be a term understood quickly enough. It will enable you to pass to your heirs up to $1.2 million *free of Federal Estate Taxes*.

There are two ways to do this. The most commonly utilized forms of the "His-and-Hers Trust" are described below.

ONE FORM OF HIS-AND-HERS TRUST

In the usual form of the "His-and-Hers Trust," you and your spouse establish *one* Revocable Living Trust with special "His-and-Hers" provisions.

Upon the death of the first spouse, two separate "His-and-Hers Trusts" will be established. The assets of the husband are transferred (retitled) to the "His Trust," the wife's assets to the "Hers Trust." This establishes two separate Federal Estate Taxable entities. Two such entities are entitled to two $600,000 exemptions for a total exemption of $1.2 million. The deceased spouse's Trust becomes an *Irrevocable* Trust at that point. Also, the value of that part of the estate is "frozen" for Federal Estate Tax purposes at that point.

Subsequently, when the second spouse dies, the assets of both Trusts, up to $600,000 each (using the frozen value of the first estate), will pass to the named Beneficiaries free of Federal Estate Taxes. And since these assets were owned by means of a Revocable Living Trust, there will be no Probate, either.

ANOTHER FORM OF HIS-AND-HERS TRUST

The second way of utilizing this method of Federal Estate Tax reduction is to establish the two parts of the "His-and-Hers Trust" now. This would require establishing two separate Trusts, with both a "wall" separating them and a special linkage joining the two Trusts. Retitling of assets would be done for both Trusts now. Although the results will be the same as using the first method, there are three strong reasons to prefer the second method. They are the following:

1. You need to go through the retitling process only once.
2. There will be no need for additional attorney's fees at the death of the first spouse.
3. There will be no confusion as to intentions regard-

ing specific assets at the time of death of the first spouse.

A CASE STUDY

Ken and Lynn Manson have been married for about 30 years. They have amassed an estate worth approximately $750,000, which they own jointly.

They looked at a chart of Federal Estate Taxes, as in Figure 10. They observed that if they did no estate planning and took no other action, their Federal Estate Tax bill at their deaths would come to $55,500. They calculated this by subtracting the tax saved on the exemption, $192,800, from the scheduled tax due of $248,300.

Naturally, they want to preserve as much of their hard-earned estate as possible for their son, Norman, and their daughter, Olivia. Obviously, Ken and Lynn want to avoid having their estate reduced by more than $55,000 in Federal Estate Taxes.

So they established "His-and-Hers Trusts," using the second method. (See Figure 11.)

When they put their checking account in one Trust, the bank told them, "One Trustee. Only one signature is accepted." Well, all they did was establish a Simple Power of Attorney for each account at each financial institution (bank, savings and loan, brokerage house, etc.).

This gave them the same freedom they had before when either could sign checks, roll over CDs, trade stocks, and so forth. Each institution provided this routine form permitting one spouse to give the other spouse current authority to take action legally, just as could be done before.

Doing this kept all their assets out of Probate and free from Federal Estate Taxes, too.

FIGURE 11

KEN MANSON
HIS TRUST $400,000
SHE'S SUCCESSOR TRUSTEE.
LYNN MANSON
HER TRUST $350,000
HE'S SUCCESSOR TRUSTEE.
KEN DIES,
HIS TRUST CONTINUES.
LYNN SURVIVES,
HAS ACCESS TO
INCOME AND
ASSETS IN BOTH
TRUSTS.
KEN'S TRUST
LATER ON,
LYNN DIES.
SON NORMAN MANSON AND DAUGHTER OLIVIA MANSON,
ACCORDING TO TERMS OF THE HIS-AND-HERS TRUSTS,
INHERIT THE ASSETS, SHARING EQUALLY BETWEEN
BROTHER AND SISTER. NOT SHARING: PROBATE,
FEDERAL ESTATE TAXES.

Figure 11 assumes that Norman dies first, because wives so frequently outlive their husbands. The same process works when the wife predeceases her husband.

Although the joint estate wasn't divided exactly in half, it really doesn't matter because the objective here is to get each part below the $600,000 exemption.

The surviving spouse still has access to the other's Trust income while still alive. The surviving spouse will have access to the deceased spouse's Trust assets only after the surviving spouse depletes the assets in his or her own Trust. And after the death of both, assets will be distributed according to the terms of the Trust. They will be distributed with reduced or no Estate Taxes, no Probate fees and more quickly than otherwise.

Another use of the "His-and-Hers Trust" is in second marriages, especially when there are children or other family members involved. It is a means of assuring both spouses that assets will go where intended.

Chapter 6
Estate Planning for Singles with Estates Over $600,000, and For Married Couples with Estates Over $1.2 Million

"The marvel of all history is the patience with which men and women submit to burdens unnecessarily laid upon them by their governments."
—William E. Borah, Speaker in U.S. Senate

"Render therefore unto Caesar the things which are Caesar's and unto God the things which are God's."
—New Testament, *Matthew, XXII, 21*

"But," you say, "my estate is larger than the limit protected by the Revocable Living Trust ($600,000 single person, $1.2 million married couple). What's a person to do?"

Remember, Federal Estate Taxes

1. Must be paid
2. In cash
3. Within nine months of death

How can these taxes be paid?

A - *Cash on Hand*. This costs exactly 100 cents on the dollar. If the tax bill is relatively small—a few thousand dollars, say—this may be the way to pay the bill. After all, that amount of money might be available in a checking account or money market fund. But if the amount is substantial, and Federal Estate Tax brackets do move up very quickly as you saw in Figure 10, then insufficient funds may be available.

B - *Liquidate Assets*. This typically will cost a little more than 100 cents on the dollar. There may be real estate or stock brokerage fees involved, possibly appraisal and other costs. Also, if the potential buyer knows this is a "Forced Sale," he or she will not offer top dollar. Furthermore, a "Forced Sale" may be at a time when market values are down. Yes, this can cost a lot more than 100 cents per dollar.

C - *Borrow Money*. This method also will cost more than 100 cents on the dollar. But a timely sale of assets may be impractical or impossible, especially if real estate or business interests are involved. Appraisal fees, interest costs and other charges can cause this method to cost substantially more than 100 cents on the dollar.

D - *Discounted Dollars*. It could cost as little as five cents to 25 cents on the dollar to pay the estate tax. Obviously, any money not paid to the government is money reaching your heirs. Why should the Federal government be your largest Beneficiary?

Discounted dollars make use of a special concept called Life Insurance—but not the traditional Life Insurance where Dad goes out to work and carries Life Insurance to provide for Mom and the kids in case he should die. That's a useful purpose, of course, but here we're discussing Federal Estate Taxes.

Now we know that "Life Insurance" is considered an unpleasant phrase by some. Still, it has a place. It can preserve a significant portion of your estate for your heirs, however, if used appropriately. Let's see how.

Let's look at Quincy and Paula Richards, ages 65 and 60, respectively. They've worked hard and invested wisely. They want to leave equal shares of their estate, after they're gone, to their four children: Stan, Tom, Uriah and Vern.

Their taxable estate is $2 million. Federal Estate Taxes come to about $700,000, or 35 percent of the total.

If Quincy and Paula do nothing, the Federal government, at 35 percent, would be the largest Beneficiary of their estate, leaving only 65 percent for the boys. Is there a less expensive way? You bet there is! (Hint-Life Insurance.)

Wait a moment. If Quincy is insured and dies, his policy pays off, but no Federal Estate Taxes are due at that time. (If Paula dies first, the reverse is also true.)

There's a relatively new form of Life Insurance available called **Survivorship**, or **Second-To-Die**, Life Insurance. It insures a married couple, but pays off only after both spouses are deceased...in time for Federal Estate Taxes.

Quincy and Paula bought a Survivorship policy with $700,000 coverage—total premium $15,000 per year for eight years for a grand total of $120,000 (8 x $15,000). The total cost of $120,000 is only 6 percent of $2 million.

No matter which way you look at it, 6 percent is less than 35 percent, or $120,000 is less than $700,000.

Yes, premiums for Quincy and Paula of $120,000 *can* buy $700,000 of coverage. That will result in preserving more assets for their children.

As of this writing only a few insurance companies carry this type of policy. But it is available. Furthermore, Survivorship policies cost less than insuring both husband and wife separately.

Of course, the concept of Survivorship Insurance doesn't help a single individual, but the *concept of using Life Insurance* as a means of preserving estate values still makes sense. It might be a little more or less costly, but it will still cost *less* than 100 cents on the dollar.

Doesn't the face value of insurance owned count in the total value of Quincy and Paula's estate? In Chapter 5, it was established that indeed, it does. Then the Quincy and Paula Richards taxable estate appears to total $2,700,000 — it looks like they'll need more insurance.

There is a solution. The $700,000 policy is counted in Quincy and Paula's estate *only if they own it*. How can they be covered and not own the policy? There are two ways. (Both would work for single persons, incidentally.)

Solution 1 - Quincy and Paula could have the policy owned by Stan, Tom, Uriah and Vern. Quincy and Paula would still be insured, and their four children would be Beneficiaries of the policy, and the policy *is not part of the Quincy and Paula Richards estate.*

Solution 2 - Let's say that the four boys have Federal Estate Tax problems of their own. Consequently, it isn't practical for them to own the policy as it would increase the value of their estates.

Quincy and Paula still can use the concept if they don't own the policy. Therefore, they need to have someone else own the policy.

Before buying this policy, Quincy and Paula met with their attorney who *created* a legal, artificial person, called an **Irrevocable Life Insurance Trust**. This special Trust will then buy and own the policy which insures Quincy and Paula, with the four children as Beneficiaries.

After Quincy and Paula are both gone, the boys will receive the $700,000 policy proceeds:

A - Free of Probate

B - Free of income taxes (Life Insurance proceeds are not subject to income taxes)

C - Free of estate taxes. An Irrevocable Trust doesn't

die. Therefore, no Federal Estate Taxes will be charged. (See Figure 12.)

There are other Irrevocable Trusts, too. The variables and complexities are too lengthy for this discussion. Suffice it to say that they apply to more advanced estate planning strategies.

As mentioned in Chapter 5, owning Life Insurance in your own name may not be the best estate planning strategy. Estates valued in excess of $1 million, not including the face value of Life Insurance, can also use the Irrevocable Life Insurance Trust to reduce the taxable estate. Many Life Insurance professionals commit a cardinal sin by placing large Life Insurance policies in an estate without considering the potential impact of Estate Taxes. Before you purchase a new policy, or when you review your current program, be sure to keep this concept in mind.

FIGURE 12

QUINCY RICHARDS
PAULA RICHARDS
SURVIVORSHIP POLICY
QUINCY and PAULA
IF, SAY, QUINCY DIES AND PAULA SURVIVES, THE POLICY CONTINUES IN FORCE.
TRUST
POLICY
IF AN IRREVOCABLE LIFE INSURANCE TRUST OWNS THE SURVIVORSHIP POLICY, THEN AFTER QUINCY AND PAULA ARE BOTH DECEASED, THE POLICY PAYS OUT TO THE FOUR BOYS FREE OF PROBATE, FREE OF INCOME TAXES, FREE FROM FEDERAL ESTATE TAXES, BUT IN TIME FOR FEDERAL ESTATE TAXES DUE ON THE REMAINDER OF THE ESTATE.
STAN
TOM
URIAH
VERN

Chapter 7
Retitling

"What's in a name? That which we call a rose by any other name, would smell as sweet;"

—Shakespeare, *Romeo and Juliet, II,2*

"A good name is better than precious ointment."

—Old Testament, *Ecclesiastes, VII, 2*

If you've decided to use the Revocable Living Trust to avoid the costs, delays and publicity of Probate and Conservatorships, you've done yourself and those about whom you care a big favor. But, while you've taken a big step in the right direction, you must take a second step, *after* your Trust is established, to implement the *plan* outlined in your documents. This step is called *retitling*.

RETITLING

Retitling, in essence, is the process of transferring your assets which are titled in your name(s) into your Revocable Living Trust. This is analogous to placing your assets into a box. The box is empty until you place your assets into it. Your Revocable Living Trust is likewise empty until you retitle your assets. It is called an Unfunded Trust as long as it is empty.

In other words, any assets which are not retitled are *not* protected by your Trust. If you don't retitle, don't establish a Revocable Living Trust. It would be of no value.

We were having lunch with a prominent CPA, and were discussing Revocable Living Trusts. He told us he'd established his some five or six years previously. When we asked him if he'd had any problems retitling his assets, his face went blank, and he said, "Retitling?" in a shocked voice. "My attorney told me nothing about retitling," he added.

His Revocable Living Trust was empty. Needless to say, that omission was quickly rectified. That one lunch saved his family tens of thousands of dollars. (And we still paid for the lunch!)

Experts in estate planning report that situation being repeated frequently over the years. A Revocable Living Trust is established, but some or even *all* assets simply are not retitled.

You must retitle assets after you've established your Revocable Living Trust to be sure they will avoid Probate and Conservatorships. It's best to begin transferring assets into your Revocable Living Trust as soon as you possibly can after your Trust is established. (See Figure 13.)

Retitling simply is showing your Revocable Living Trust as the owner of your assets. Of course, as Trustee, you continue to control the assets, but you do so in the name of the Trust.

You will continue to pay your *income taxes* the same way almost as if the Revocable Living Trust were invisible. No separate income tax filing is necessary. Certain *other* types of Trusts may be required to file separate income tax returns using Form 1041, but this does not apply to your Revocable Living Trust.

But you did successfully remove these assets from Probate and Conservatorship.

Remember, however, it it necessary to have your name appear the same way on *ALL* legal documents.

John Smith and Mary Smith established a Joint (under

FIGURE 13

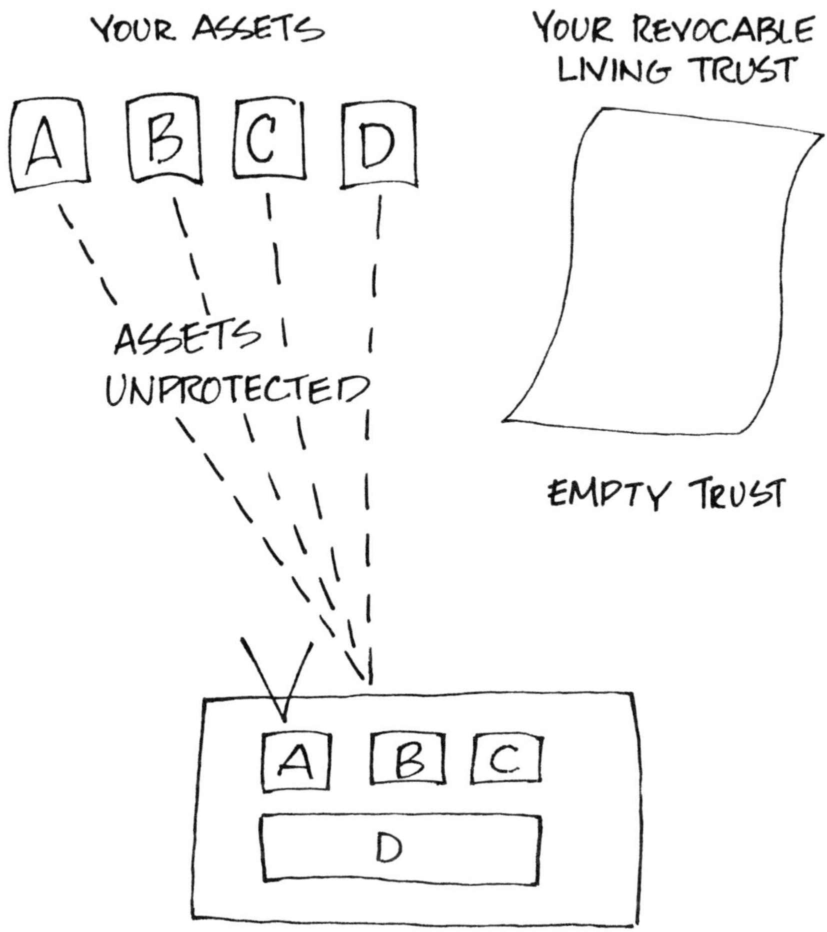

ASSETS A, B, C, AND D ARE NOW PROTECTED. THEY'VE BEEN RETITLED.

$600,000) Revocable Living Trust on October 29, 1990. Assets will be retitled to read as follows. There will be some variation from institution to institution.

John Smith and Mary Smith TTEEs
John and Mary Smith Trust
UTD 10/29/90

TTEEs means Trustees.

UTD means Under Trust Dated.

Some institutions will substitute UAD (Under Agreement Dated) for UTD.

Chapter 8
Bank, Savings and Loans and Credit Union Accounts

"Who steals my purse steals trash."
—Shakespeare, *Othello, III,3*

"Put not your trust in money, but put your money in trust."
—O.W. Holmes, *The Autocrat of the Breakfast Table*

So many people have assets in Banks, Savings and Loan Associations and Credit Union Accounts that further discussions of these institutions will provide more perspective. Consider the assets owned by a married couple, Walt and Xaviera Young. Their two sons' names are Zeb and Al. If they own an account at a Bank, Savings and Loan or Credit Union, it will be subject to Probate if it is entitled:

A -Walt Young and
Xaviera Young
OR
B - Walt Young
Xaviera Young

Either of the above titles **WILL** *cause the assets to be Probated on the death of either Walt or Xaviera.*

AVOID PROBATE

Assuming no Revocable Living Trust exists, any of the following titles will **AVOID** Probate temporarily on the death of either party:

I - Walt Young or
Xaviera Young
II - Walt Young
Xaviera Young JTWROS
(JTWROS = Joint Survivors with Rights of Survivorship)
III - Walt Young
Xaviera Young Tenancy By the Entirety
IV - Walt Young or
Xaviera Young
In Trust For
Zeb Young and Al Young
V - Walt Young or
Xaviera Young
P.O.D. Zeb Young
VI - Walt Young or
Xaviera Young
T.O.D. Zeb Young
and Al Young

If you use any of these titles for your account, you won't truly *avoid* Probate; you'll be *delaying* it. Nonetheless, be sure that your account statements show the complete and correct title registration. In case questions arise and the account registration form cannot be located, the account statements will answer those questions.

The weaknesses of Joint Tenancy were examined at some length, so it's not necessary to spend much time on Registrations I, II and III above.

For Banks, Savings and Loans and Credit Unions, however, there is an additional disadvantage to Walt and Xaviera in Joint Tenancy. If either should have written a bad check on *any* account at that same institution, the institution can offset the debit in one account by removing money from another. That's another reason the illustrations did not show sons Zeb and/or Al as joint owners in the formats under discussion.

IN TRUST FOR

Registration IV, "In Trust For," is not generally well known. This is a method of designating the Beneficiary to your account(s) without actually creating a Trust. Usually your signature card will suffice, or the institution will accept use of the phrase "In Trust For." This is sometimes abbreviated I.T.F.

However, you must never name a minor or incompetent adult as Beneficiary or Joint Owner. Such people have no legal right to receive or own such assets—nor the legal capacity to sign contracts. A court usually must assign a Guardian or Custodian to act for the incompetent person.

Most institutions will permit you to use I.T.F. This is sometimes called "The Totten Trust" because the first recorded use of this format was by a person named Totten.

Some states have inheritance taxes. Some of those states will "freeze" a joint account, but usually not an account registered "In Trust For."

PAYMENT ON DEATH

Registration V "Payment On Death" appears frequently abbreviated as P.O.D. on documents.

P.O.D. is not available in all states. Furthermore, in those states where P.O.D. is legal, not all financial institutions recognize its use.

The use of P.O.D. permits you to designate a Beneficiary. If your state permits it, it will enable you to designate a Beneficiary for your account, *temporarily* avoiding Probate.

Regarding both I.T.F. and P.O.D., most institutions will permit more than one name as Beneficiary on "In Trust For" and only one name on "Payment On Death." When you use more than one name, use *"and"* and not *"or."*

TRANSFER ON DEATH

Registration VI, "T.O.D.," is an abbreviation for "Transfer On Death." As of this writing, it is available only in a few states. It works similarly to "P.O.D.," but unlike P.O.D., T.O.D. can be used on other types of assets, including real estate. In addition, T.O.D. specifically permits more than onc named Beneficiary.

However, there is a flaw in the use of T.O.D., as illustrated in the Young family. They've named sons Zeb and Al on their account, thus:

Walt Young or
Xaviera Young
T.O.D. Zeb Young
and Al Young

which we've shown as Registration VII, indicating a desire by Walt and Xaviera for their sons to share *equally*. T.O.D. will not allow for anything other than equal sharing. If Walt and Xaviera have any other formula in mind, T.O.D. simply won't work.

Nonetheless, if Walt and Xaviera intend for one son to get all if the other dies, T.O.D. *may not do that*.

If Walt, Xaviera and Zeb die together in a common accident, or if Zeb predeceases Walt and Xaviera, *Zeb's share will go to his living descendants*, to be shared equally among them. If there are none, only then will Zeb's share go to Al.

LOOK AT THE REVOCABLE LIVING TRUST

The various methods of trying to avoid Probate have been described because they are so widely used, so widely believed in, and so inadequate for their intended purpose—avoiding Probate. Of course, management of assets during incapacity isn't addressed at all; so none of these methods helps there.

The Revocable Living Trust will handle all these problems. It will do so simply, easily, and inexpensively.

The appropriate registration would look like this:

VII - Walt Young and Xaviera Young TTEEs
Walt and Xaviera Young Trust
UTD 1/3/90

If Xaviera were a single person, then her registration would say:

VIII - Xaviera Young TTEE of
Xaviera Young Trust
UTD 1/3/90

The designations TTEE and TTEES are abbreviations of Trustee and Trustees, respectively.

UTD stands for Under Trust Dated and is followed by the date the Trust was established. Sometimes UAD (Under Agreement Dated) is used in lieu of UTD, with essentially the same meaning. Again, the precise format of titles will vary by institution.

If Walt and Xaviera Young retitle their bank accounts

on January 3, 1990, the title would appear as Registration VII.

What's involved in accomplishing this? Walt and Xaviera need to go to the bank with a copy of their Revocable Living Trust and sign new forms. Some banks will assign new account numbers; the clerks can explain what's involved. The procedure can be completed in less than ten minutes.

Many credit unions, usually federally chartered, cannot handle a Trust account because of regulations limiting them to "Natural Persons." You may need to designate your Beneficiaries there by another method. Discuss this with your credit union representative.

CHECKING ACCOUNTS

A few words about checking accounts. As you know, with a joint account, any named party can sign checks.

If you use Registration VII, then any Trustee can sign. If you retitle your account in this manner, *you do not have to show the Trust name on your checks*. The checks are not assets; actually, they're liabilities.

Walt and Xaviera originally had their checks printed like this:

Walt Young
Xaviera Young

They continued to use the same checks because their bank let them continue to use the old account number. Even if they'd had to change the account number, their checks would still read as above.

If your bank insists that the Trust name appear on your checks, thereby announcing to the world that you have a

Trust, then consider using another bank. Your Yellow Pages can help you locate another bank, and a telephone call will determine if they can accommodate your need.

Retitling a Certificate of Deposit is *not* the same as cashing it in. There should be no penalty for doing so. Discusss this with your institution.

On July 29, 1990, new Federal regulations regarding insurance coverage were implemented. If *all* your accounts total over $100,000, be sure to discuss the new rules with your representative there.

Chapter 9
Real Estate

"The power of perpetuating our properties in our families is one of the most valuable and interesting circumstances belonging to it, and that which tends the most to the perpetuation of society itself."

—Edmund Burke, *Reflections on the Revolution in France*

"And ye shall eat the fat of the land."

—Old Testament, *Genesis, XLC, 18*

Whenever a list of the richest people in America is published, the data reveals that the great majority of those people has substantial real estate holdings. (See *Forbes* magazine's annual list, for instance.)

Furthermore, many Americans of more modest means own their own homes; some own additional properties as well.

In addition, some hold mortgages on still other pieces of real estate.

Suffice it to say, then, that real estate represents a large asset owned by many Americans. Real estate laws are extremely strict, reflecting the importance of real estate both to individuals and to society in general.

One way of keeping real estate out of Probate *temporarily* is to title it in Joint Ownership. There are many reasons *not* to use this method, discussed earlier for the most part. But there are several special applications for real estate.

Firstly, real estate titled in Joint Tenancy with Right of

Survivorship (JTWROS) will have deeds appearing like this:

Ben Casey and
Darlene Casey

It's important to note the use of "and" because real estate does not use "or" in its title. It is considered "pure" joint ownership.

To sell the above real estate both Ben and Darlene must sign; if one dies, the survivor must provide a Death Certificate and other documents to complete the sale. If one is *disabled* (incapacitated), how could that person sign? A Conservatorship or Guardianship would need to be established and administered by a judge. This is typically a Probate Court judge. There's the Probate situation again!

Of course, once Ben and Darlene are both gone, the property goes to Probate. Adding children's names may cause even more problems, as was discussed in Chapter 2.

In addition to potential gift taxes and penalties, which are compounded and can add up very quickly, state inheritance taxes may become a factor, too.

Although a surviving spouse enjoys an unlimited marital deduction resulting in no tax liability, a nontaxable inheritance tax return should be filed in those states that do have inheritance taxes.

In some situations, the surviving Joint Tenant may be entitled to a new income tax basis in part of the property, and the new basis can be determined based on the fair market value of the property at the time of death as reported on the nontaxable inheritance tax return.

Joint Tenancy *may* be subject to inheritance tax liability. You could be in for an unpleasant surprise by having to pay not only the inheritance tax, but also additional penalties and interest for late reporting. This varies by state.

Ben and Darlene considered using a *Durable Power of Attorney*. Their real estate agent rightly advised against it because potential buyers would likely indicate lack of confidence in their ability to deliver "clear title" to the property. This is because an outstanding Durable Power of Attorney sometimes is deemed to cloud the issue. A Revocable Living Trust is a lot easier and simpler.

LIFE ESTATE

Financial situations sometimes involve the concept of "retain a life estate" in certain property.

This gives you the right to live in, use and enjoy this property for the rest of your life so that you cannot outlive it. The property, however, is owned by somebody else.

Of course, if you don't own it, you can't sell it, rent it, or borrow money against it. It isn't yours. Not infrequently this is used as an attempt to reduce the size of an estate for Federal Estate Tax purposes. It also could be used to prevent a spouse from obtaining ownership of such property.

Obviously a Revocable Living Trust will enable you to accomplish the same thing. A big *disadvantage* to retaining a life estate is that not only do you give up control of the property, but also *there may be gift tax and income tax* implications, too. If you consider using the life estate, be sure to talk to an experienced CPA or tax attorney before you decide.

UNRECORDED DEED

Occasionally an individual uses an *Unrecorded Deed* as

a means of avoiding Probate and simplifying the transfer of real estate.

The Unrecorded Deed is made to another party, or to a Trust, but is not recorded until after the death of the original owner(s). Of course, the original owner can change his or her mind and simply destroy the Unrecorded Deed.

Again, there may be gift tax, estate tax and income tax implications. Furthermore, your state may have certain restrictions on use of the Unrecorded Deed. Such restrictions *could invalidate* this method or restrict it so as to make this approach useless. Check your state's statutes if you are considering this technique.

Yet another means of invalidating the Unrecorded Deed is: what happens if the deed is lost, stolen or destroyed accidentally? The answer is obvious—this method won't work, since the deed is unrecorded. If you do consider this, be sure to enlist the assistance of highly competent legal and tax advice.

Of course, if you have a Revocable Living Trust, your objectives will more easily be accomplished. The deed then would be titled like this:

Frank N. Stein TTEE
For the Frank N. Stein
Trust UTD 1/24/90 **(single owner)**

or

Charles Khan and
Sharon Khan TTEES of
The Charles and Sharon
Kahn Trust UTD 2/14/90 **(married couple)**

The precise format differs by state. The above formats are for illustrative purposes only.

When it comes to joint ownership by two or more *unmarried* individuals, there's a special danger.

Take the case of two sisters, Anne and Margaret. They decide to invest in a rental property to be owned jointly (JTWROS). They each put up 50 percent of the cost and each derives 50 percent of the benefits of owning such property.

If one sister died, the rental property would not then go through Probate and the surviving sister would own *the entire property*. In this scenario, the deceased sister's family unfortunately would be *disinherited* by this action. (See Figure 14.)

Because both families were establishing Revocable Living Trusts, each sister inserted her *one-half undivided interest* into the Trust, and retitled real estate to reflect that. That was easily said and easily done. You can place separate ownership interests in more than one Trust.

PARTIAL OWNERSHIP

Also, when a person indicates a *partial ownership* in a property and wants to put that part into his or her Trust, you again use the phrase "undivided interest."

If, let's say, five persons each own one-fifth of a property, each owns a one-fifth (or 20 percent) *undivided interest* in that property. (If you own one-fifth of a cow, or a horse, or a deck of cards, or a factory, you own an "undivided interest." You can't divide that ownership.)

If a person wants to place his or her fractional ownership in a Revocable Living Trust, that person retitles his or her fractional undivided interest.

FIGURE 14

ANNE
MARGARET
PROPERTY OWNED IN JOINT TENANCY WITH RIGHTS OF SURVIVORSHIP.
IF ANNE DIES,
MARGARET AS SURVIVOR OWNS THE RENTAL PROPERTY IN ITS ENTIRETY.
THE PROPERTY DOES NOT GO THROUGH PROBATE, BUT ANNE'S HALF DOES NOT GO TO ANNE'S FAMILY. THIS IS AN EXPENSIVE WAY TO AVOID PROBATE.

MORTGAGES AND NOTES

Mortgages and promissory notes also can be jointly owned, or owned by a Revocable Living Trust. A mortgage is legal evidence of debt. Some call it an I.O.U.

Mortgages and notes typically have a fixed rate of interest for a fixed period of time. Mortgages and promissory notes have *resale values*, and such values fluctuate in response to interest rate changes. Because of such fluctuations in value, it is *vital* to avoid Probate.

In reality, the sale of real estate or mortgages could be a "forced sale" and could occur at a bad time. The market could move against the seller, and an alert buyer will not offer the best price if he or she knows of or senses a forced sale.

Many mortgages include a "Due on Sale" clause. Before retitling your real estate for your Revocable Living Trust, which is *not* a sale, be sure to discuss this with your mortgage holder. This will avoid any unnecessary complications.

Also, be sure to use a document called a *Quit-Claim Deed* to transfer title to your Revocable Living Trust. Do *not* use a Warranty Deed or a Bill of Sale. A Quit-Claim Deed transfers interest in real estate, but it is not evidence of a sale. Consequently, the Due on Sale clause in your mortgage is not triggered. In addition, there are *no* income tax or property tax implications involved in using this document.

The Quit-Claim Deed is registered in your county courthouse with the County Recorder of Deeds.

Chapter 10
Stocks, Bonds, Mutual Funds and Stock Brokerage Accounts

"Do you know the only thing which gives me pleasure? It's to see my dividends coming in."

—John D. Rockefeller (*Winkler, John D.*)

"There are two times in a man's life when he should not speculate: when he can't afford it, and when he can."

—Mark Twain, *Pudd'nhead Wilson's Calendar*

Unfortunately the great majority of brokerage accounts are titled with one individual's name or, in the case of a married couple, Joint Tenancy With Right of Survivorship (JTWROS).

It would be much better if more accounts were entitled in the name of a Revocable Living Trust.

In the past, when a married couple would open an account, it was automatically assumed they wanted JTWROS, similar to such people at banks, savings and loans, real estate agencies, insurance companies and other financial institutions. As you have no doubt concluded, that assumption is no longer automatically made.

What most of the public doesn't know, and many financial professionals forget, is that a JTWROS brokerage account is *"and,"* not *"or."* If your financial adviser knows that one of the spouses is incapacitated, brokerage account transactions must cease unless a Durable Power of Attorney is available.

When one spouse dies, the account should be retitled promptly. Your brokerage firm can assist you with this function.

Central asset accounts, which combine features of checking accounts with brokerage accounts, *appear* to be in the form of "*or*," but this, strictly speaking, applies only to the checkwriting privileges. (Either spouse legally can write checks.)

The use of "In Trust For" and "P.O.D." and "T.O.D." designations, available at banks, savings and loans and credit unions, is not permitted at brokerage houses.

Therefore, JTWROS is available to delay Probate, and the Revocable Living Trust is available to *avoid* Probate.

Many people take delivery of certificates, which they then keep in safe deposit boxes. The title designations on these certificates are the same as at brokerage houses.

It is wiser to keep your securities on deposit at the brokerage house for several reasons:

1. Simpler record keeping. Your statement, typically monthly, will show all transactions for the recording period, including interest, dividends, and stock splits.

2. The central asset type of account automatically "sweeps" such interest or dividend payments into a money market fund. You typically can access these funds by writing a check, using a *debit card* (you use a debit card as you would a charge card, but the computer *debits* your account, removing that sum of money from it), or both. (See Figure 15.)

3. Most such account statements will show year-to-date figures, too. If you do any income planning or tax planning (especially if you file quarterly estimated tax payments), this surely simplifies your life.

4. While there may be a fee associated with your account, it's worth a small charge for the service provided.

Ed and Fern Gallagher own 25 stocks, and keep the certificates in their home safe.

FIGURE 15

HOW A CENTRAL ASSETS ACCOUNT WORKS.

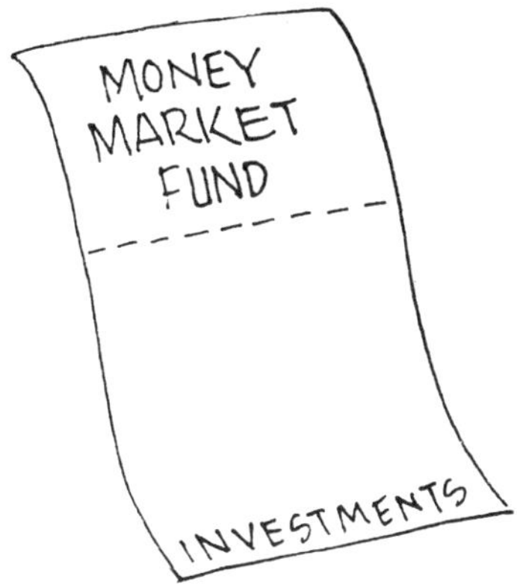

IT'S ONE ACCOUNT WITH TWO INTERACTING PARTS.

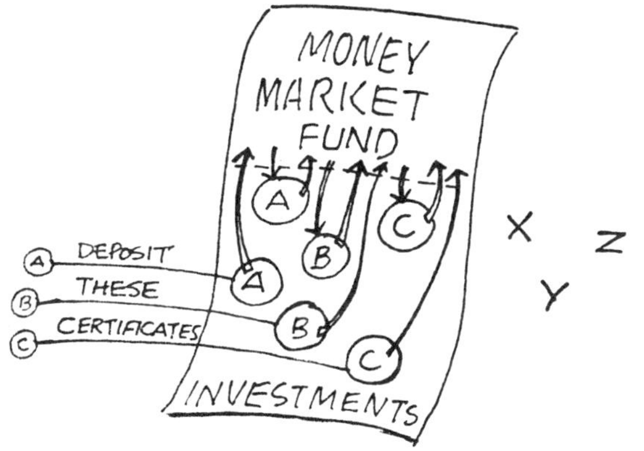

MONEY LEAVES THE MONEY MARKET FUND TO MAKE INVESTMENTS, IF ANY (X, Y, AND Z), AND INTEREST, DIVIDENDS, SALE PROCEEDS, MATURING PRINCIPAL - ANY FUNDS - AUTOMATICALLY GO TO THE MONEY MARKET FUND FROM ALL INVESTMENTS.

TYPICALLY, ACCESS TO THE MONEY MARKET FUND IS VIA CHECK AND DEBIT CARD ("PLASTIC CHECK") - SOME ACCOUNTS OFFER ADDITIONAL METHODS OF ACCESS.

Each stock pays quarterly dividends—therefore, 100 checks a year come to the Gallaghers' home.

Each stock files and sends them a Form 1099 in January, and their CPA must process all 25 Form 1099's. The CPA charges for services based on time used.

Over the years, the Gallaghers have moved a few times, necessitating 25 notices, one to each company.

Over the years, the Gallaghers have had stock splits, delayed or lost dividends checks and tender offers, from time to time.

The Gallaghers, an older couple, met with their financial advisers shortly after their neighbors' house had been burgled; the home safe had been forced open and documents removed.

They were discussing the safety of leaving their stocks on deposit with a brokerage firm after reviewing the four main points listed above.

They learned that the firm was a member of the Securities Investor Protection Corporation (SIPC), which is a quasi-governmental organization.

The SIPC was created by Congress under the Securities Investor Protection Act of 1970; the law was amended in 1978 and 1980.

The *function* of SIPC is *similar* to that of the FDIC in terms of protecting the safety of clients' accounts in case of the bankruptcy of the brokerage firm.

Customers of a failed firm will receive *all securities* registered in their names, or in the process of being registered in their names, *without limit*.

In addition, SIPC funds are available to satisfy *any shortfall*, up to a maximum of *$500,000*, including a maximum of *$100,000* for claims made for cash.

The SIPC is funded by revenues from brokers and dealers which are required by law to be members of the SIPC.

The SIPC isn't a U.S. Government Agency, even though Congress created it. It does, however, have a $1 billion line of credit with the U.S. Treasury if the SIPC Fund should turn out to be insufficient.

Most member firms feel that $500,000 is insufficient insurance coverage and have made arrangements for additional, private insurance. Some central asset accounts have as much as $10 to $25 million total insurance.

The Gallaghers, upon learning this, were very interested in the insurance coverage.

They also were interested in investments in tax-free income provided by municipal bonds.

Many municipal bonds issued since 1987 are in "book-entry" form. That is, there are no certificates created for many issues. Requiring certificates means clients cannot buy such issues.

Furthermore, most municipal bonds (and corporate bonds) are *callable*. This means that the issuer, on a prearranged schedule, can call bonds back, typically for refinancing. But some bondholders don't receive notice on a timely basis. In fact, on the old coupon-bearing "Bearer" bonds, the issuer has nobody to notify. That means the investor could lose six months' worth of interest if he or she doesn't collect principal on a timely basis.

On the other hand, if the bond is held in a brokerage account, the bond principal is received and credited to a client's account promptly. And if it's a central assets account, the money received is swept into an interest-bearing money market fund and begins earning interest.

Let's get back to Ed and Fern Gallagher. The 25 stocks they owned and held were "JTWROS" and they understood that the death of one would enable the survivor to own all the stocks, and without going through Probate. They asked how to handle paperwork in the event one died.

Well, the survivor has to contact all 25 companies, or their banks acting as transfer agents, providing 25 death certificates, 25 affidavits of domicile, 25 tax waivers, and 25 of any other documents required.

If the same stocks were in a brokerage account, then only *one set of documents* would suffice. The brokerage firm would handle it for them.

Many brokerage clients, the Gallaghers among them, would ask why firms preferred that they leave certificates on deposit.

In addition to the reasons enumerated above, it simplifies everybody's recordkeeping, making it easier for their financial advisers to track and analyze their investments. Full-service brokers believe in *service,* which requires a lot of behind-the-scenes review and analysis.

Furthermore, if a client wants to sell part or all of an investment, that can be done via telephone—*from anywhere in the world.* They needn't worry about running back and forth to home safes or safe deposit boxes. (Most brokers have many out-of-town clients, as well as some who live outside the United States, and several who travel frequently. As you can see, this becomes an important factor.) If it's simpler, if it's easier, financial professionals generally prefer to do it that way. And so do most people.

If you've got questions about the advisability of leaving certificates on deposit with a brokerage firm, discuss them with your stockbroker.

MUTUAL FUNDS

Mutual funds are pools of money, representing investments by many people. Typically, there are millions, or even *billions,* of dollars in them.

"No-Load" mutual funds have no commission charges. (Ask No-Load fund representative about *ALL* expenses, represented by the *expense ratio*. "No-Load" is not free.) A No-Load fund is sold to the public directly by the fund. These shares typically cannot be held by a brokerage firm, but can be held by the mutual fund firm.

Those funds which are "Front-Load" (commissions charged at the time of purchase) or "Contingent, Deferred Back-End Load" (a commission or redemption fee *may* be charged, based on certain contingencies, which vary somewhat from fund to fund) usually *can* be held at a brokerage firm, even one which doesn't sell that fund. If in doubt, ask your stockbroker regarding any fund you own, and whether it can be held at his or her firm.

There are many other types of investments—U.S. Government Obligations, Limited Partnerships, Brokerage CD's, Zero-Coupon Bonds, Unit Investment Trusts. The list is very long.

Generally speaking, it is wiser—certainly simpler and easier—to leave investments on deposit with a brokerage firm.

RETITLING

When you retitle your investments after establishing your Revocable Living Trust, you will see it's much easier to do so with a brokerage account. It's done by retitling *the account* rather than retitling each investment one at a time. The brokerage firm will do most of the work for you.

By the way, if you don't want to leave certificates on deposit at a brokerage firm, you still can get help from your broker in retitling securities. You can *temporarily* deposit the certificates and ask the firm to issue new certificates for you. There may be a service charge, which frequently is reduced or eliminated for good customers. Be sure to ask beforehand. Trying to retitle investments yourself is time-consuming and frustrating, and often leads to errors and long delays. Brokerage firms specialize in retitling assets—let them do it for you, so you can avoid Probate the easy way.

If you do want new certificates issued to you, anticipate a wait of from four to six weeks to receive all your certificates. Between Thanksgiving and New Year's Day, it may take an extra week or so to process these certificates.

Retitling assets into a Revocable Living Trust, or in order to delete a deceased owner's name, is *not* a taxable event.

By the way, it seems a lot of people don't realize how easy it is to use a brokerage account as opposed to holding certificates themselves.

There's the story of a time when an attorney came to visit his broker. His mother (a widow) had died a few weeks before, and mother and son (Sue and Cy Saw) owned a lot of stocks and bonds jointly. About two-thirds of what they owned was in a brokerage account, with the remaining one-third in the form of certificates which had been kept in a safe deposit box.

As an attorney, Cy came in prepared with an attache' case full of documents, and a second one with certificates. They handled the certificates first. Because he was prepared, it took about an hour and a half to handle that one-third.

When they finished that portion, Cy sighed and said, "Now we're really in for it. We've got two-thirds to go."

He was amazed when he saw they were finished, less than 15 minutes later!

Needless to say, Cy's certificates now are *all* on deposit

with the brokerage firm.

Some brokerage firms demand a complete copy of your Revocable Living Trust. This represents an invasion of your privacy. Lawyers have objected to this requirement, and many lawyers advise their clients against complying with it. There is at least one major Wall Street firm that is more cooperative. In respecting your privacy, they require only that you fill out and sign a simple one-page form with general information about your Trust.

Chapter 11
Retirement Plans: IRAs, Keoghs, Simplified Employee Pensions, Tax-Sheltered Annuities, 401 (k) Plans, Pensions, Profit Sharing, Employee Stock Ownership Plans, Etc.

"Rest, rest, perturbed spirit!"
—Shakespeare, *Hamlet, I, 5*

"Grow old with me!
The best is yet to be,
The last of life for which the first was made."
—Robert Browning, *Rabbi Ben Ezra*

Retirement Accounts comprise a separate category of assets, irrespective of which type of plan it is.

Although various plans have different features, including whether they are controlled by employer or by employee, many factors are common to them all.

One important common factor is the form of ownership. Ownership must be in the name of the participant.

A Retirement Plan cannot be titled in Joint Ownership. It cannot be in the name of a Revocable Living Trust. (Retirement Plans *are* Trusts.) Each participant, once vested, owns his or her plan in his or her name only. Recent changes in the law mandate full vesting in five years or less.

Retirement Plans have another factor in common. On the death of the participant, the assets will avoid Probate if there is at least one named Beneficiary available at the time of death. *Never name your estate as the Beneficiary.* If you do name your estate, assets which could avoid Probate will be subjected to Probate unnecessarily.

Retirement Plan assets are tax-deferred. Therefore, income taxes are due when assets are paid out, which typically occurs shortly after death. The spouse of the participant, if named as Beneficiary, and *only the spouse*, has a special option. He or she can roll the assets over into an IRA (which can be created for this purpose), thereby continuing to defer taxes. This important option, which permits you to utilize the valuable tax-deferral mechanism, is often overlooked by the public and by their advisers. (An employer-sponsored plan may limit the ability to pay out a lump sum.)

How then can you get the Retirement Plan assets into a Revocable Living Trust? Name your spouse (if you have one) as Primary Beneficiary, and your Revocable Living Trust as Contingent (or Secondary) Beneficiary. If you have no spouse, there's no rollover option to preserve, so just name your Revocable Living Trust as Beneficiary. But if your estate exceeds $600,000 in size, some additional estate planning may be needed. Consult an estate planning specialist about how to "freeze" a deceased spouse's Retirement Plan for estate tax planning purposes.

Note: Many plans require a Spousal Consent to change Beneficiaries. To obtain the form, just ask your Plan Administrator or Custodian. In many firms, the Employee Benefits or Personnel Department can assist you.

You may have several IRAs at different institutions. Change your Beneficiary to your spouse and your Revocable Living Trust, as mentioned above. Later, if you ever want to change Beneficiaries other than your spouse, all you need to do is change your Trust Beneficiaries.

You do not need Spousal Consent to change IRA Beneficiaries.

INCAPACITY

Look at incapacity for a moment. Hal Johnson, let's say, retired from the Dear John Company. He rolled over his Pension and 401(k) Plans into an IRA. These Plans, as it is for so many people, represent by far his largest single asset. His IRA Rollover is worth $300,000.

Hal Johnson had worked for the Dear John Company for about 30 years, beginning just after he married his wife, Inez Johnson. Inez was a housewife all that time.

Hal and Inez now, in retirement, live from Social Security payments, outside investments, and occasional withdrawals from his IRA Rollover.

Unexpectedly, Hal becomes incapacitated. In order to make some of the medical payments, Inez needs to obtain funds from the IRA Rollover. For most people, this could not be done without lengthy and costly court proceedings, possibly resulting in a Conservatorship.

Here's an instance when a Durable Power of Attorney can come in very handy.

The Durable Power of Attorney, coupled with the Hal and Inez Johnson Revocable Living Trust, enabled the Johnson family to continue its financial affairs without interruption. It took only three business days for Inez to be able to access the IRA Rollover assets. (See Figure 16.) She also can make investment decisions in the IRA Rollover.

NOTE: If a person is legally disabled, withdrawals are not subject to the 10 percent tax penalty for pre-59 1/2 withdrawals.

FIGURE 16

HAL JOHNSON
INEZ JOHNSON
IRA
ROLLOVER
MUST BE TITLED IN HAL JOHNSON'S NAME ONLY.
MONEY
HAL IS INCAPACITATED
AND INEZ NEEDS MONEY TO PAY BILLS, SHE EASILY UNLOCKS THE IRA ROLLOVER BY USING A DURABLE POWER OF ATTORNEY.
IRA ROLLOVER
DURABLE POWER OF ATTORNEY

DEATH

If Hal were to die, with Inez surviving, she retains the option to roll over his $300,000 IRA Rollover into her IRA. That continues to defer income taxes.

Eventually, though, Inez dies. Since she never remarried, she has no surviving spouse. At this point, *income taxes* are due. At 31%, Federal income tax liability comes to $93,000. There may be state income and inheritance taxes too, which could push the new total tax liability above $100,000. Assuming no Federal estate taxes are due, her heirs will see one-third *or more* of their inheritance from the IRA Rollover disappear.

The impact of this large tax bill can be reduced significantly.

Hal and Inez could set up an Irrevocable Life Insurance Trust and have it buy and own a Survivorship Life Insurance Policy. If Inez learns of this strategy after Hal's death, she could employ this technique as the only insured person. This would provide cash at *much less than 100 cents per dollar*.

And if their estate exceeded $600,000, they could merely increase their coverage to allow for *all* taxes due. The "discounted dollar" technique is discussed in greater detail in Chapter 6.

That's successful planning. Nobody plans to fail; many fail to plan.

Chapter 12
Life Insurance and Other Insurance

"Hell: being locked for all eternity in a small room with a life insurance salesman."

—Woody Allen, comedy routine

"But if any provide not for his own, and specifically for those of his own house, he hath denied the faith, and is worse than the infidel."

—New Testament, *I Timothy 5:8*

Americans buy and own Life Insurance. Of course, this is done for various reasons, including those mentioned in Chapter 5.

Irrespective of reason for purchase, Life Insurance policies have some factors in common.

For instance, there are three main positions relative to a Life Insurance policy:

1 - *Owner*. This is the person who owns, controls and is responsible for premiums on the Life Insurance policy.

2 - *Insured*. This is the person whose death calls for Life Insurance proceeds (sometimes called "Death Benefits" or "Estate Benefits") to be paid.

3 - *Beneficiary*. This is the person who receives the Life Insurance proceeds.

The owner and the insured do not have to be the same person. There are countless situations and written policies where the owner and insured are not the same. You saw an example of this in Chapter 5, when an Irrevocable Life Insurance Trust owned a policy. A more common situation is a policy owned by a married couple with a young child.

Kevin and Laura Miller have one child and heir, their son, Nate, who is a minor. He is only nine.

Kevin and Laura own the policy, and are Beneficiaries of it. (Of course, once their Revocable Living Trust is established, the Trust will become Beneficiary.)

Nate is the insured. (See Figure 17.) Why would parents insure their nine year old son?

Son Nate is young. Consequently, premiums are lower than if either Kevin or Laura were insured.

TAX-FREE BUILDUP

The annual premium paid by Kevin and Laura go partly for insurance, and partly for the investment providing tax-free buildup of wealth. Life Insurance policies, if they call for at least seven years' worth of premiums, allow access to the "inside buildup" of value on an income tax free basis. And many policies mandate little or no charge for accessing these funds.

AVOIDS PROBATE

Kevin and Laura Miller bought the policy shortly after Nate was born. Their intention is to let the values build up and then use *tax-free access to pay for college tuition*. Naturally, if Nate doesn't attend college, or even better, wins a full scholarship, Kevin and Laura will continue to let the values build up. As owners, they can use the asset for any purpose at all.

The purpose of taking out this Life Insurance policy was not for the traditional insurance purpose; rather, it was to use the tax-free buildup for some future purpose.

By the way, after establishing their Revocable

FIGURE 17

KEVIN AND LAURA HAVE TAX-FREE ACCESS TO THE INSIDE BUILD-UP OF WEALTH FOR COLLEGE TUITION OR FOR ANY PURPOSE AT ALL.

SON NATE IS YOUNG. CONSEQUENTLY, PREMIUMS ARE LOWER THAN IF EITHER KEVIN OR LAURA WERE INSURED.

Living Trust, the Millers retitled the Life Insurance Policy to place it into their Trust, *in addition* to naming the Trust as Beneficiary. The Trustees (Kevin and Laura) are empowered to access the built-up assets. If neither Kevin nor Laura can act, their Successor Trustee or Contingent Successor Trustee will act for them.

Another feature of Life Insurance policies is that *they have assets which can avoid Probate.* In order for the Life Insurance proceeds to avoid Probate, though, there must be at least one named Beneficiary available.

Do not name your estate as Beneficiary. That would put the proceeds *back into Probate.* This occurs more often than professionals care to admit. Review your policies for Beneficiaries. Also, be sure there are no minors named as Beneficiary. They legally cannot receive the assets.

SPENDTHRIFT CLAUSE

In addition, there's a little-known insurance law in all 50 states. It's called the "Spendthrift Clause."

Let's say Orin Quill ran up debts totalling $500,000, and had assets of only $250,000, and then died with a $50,000 insurance policy.

Orin Quill's creditors *cannot* attach the $50,000 Life Insurance proceeds if there is at least one named Beneficiary available. If Orin had named his estate as Beneficiary, the creditors could attach the proceeds. *NEVER* name your estate as Beneficiary for any insurance contract. (See Figure 18.)

Many people have more than one insurance policy, and events cause them to change Beneficiaries. If you name your Revocable Living Trust as Beneficiary, then you need only amend your Trust as to Beneficiaries, and you will have changed all the policies, in effect. Many

FIGURE 18

ORIN QUILL

HAS ASSETS WORTH $250,000, HAS DEBTS OF ABOUT $500,000

AND OWNS A LIFE INSURANCE CONTRACT WITH $50,000 FACE VALUE (NO CASH BUILD-UP).

IF ORIN NAMES HIS ESTATE AS BENEFICIARY, THEN ON HIS DEATH, THE $50,000 WILL

GO THROUGH PROBATE, WITH ANY REMAINING BALANCE GOING TO CREDITORS. IF HE NAMES BENEFICIARIES, HOWEVER, THE $50,000 PROCEED WILL GO DIRECTLY TO THEM.

BENEFICIARIES

people forget to change all their policies, for instance, when a Beneficiary dies. Obviously, this becomes easier for you to handle if you need to amend only one document—your Revocable Living Trust.

Remember, Life Insurance proceeds are exempt from all income taxes. They may not be exempt from estate taxes.

Other types of insurance (Disability Income, Property and Casualty, etc.) should show your Revocable Living Trust as Beneficiary, where the insurance company permits it. (You may have to request a special form—or you may need to name your Trust as the Secondary Beneficiary.) Therefore, if you're incapacitated, your Trust will continue to operate for you.

Your insurance agent, or Personnel Department for employee plans, can assist you in changing Beneficiaries.

Chapter 13
U.S. Savings Bonds: E, EE, H, HH

"Take Stock in America."
—U.S. Savings Bond Advertisement

"The land of the free and the home of the brave."
—Francis Scott Key, *The Star-Spangled Banner*

"...Government of the people, by the people, for the people..."
—Abraham Lincoln, Gettysburg Address

They used to be called Series E and Series H Bonds. Now the U.S. Government issues them as Series EE and Series HH Bonds.

The Series E and the Series EE Bonds *accumulate* interest, on a *tax-deferred* basis.

The Series H and the Series HH Bonds *pay out* interest every six months, on a *taxable* basis.

Series E Bonds can be exchanged to Series H, and EE to HH, on a basis which continues to defer income taxes on the accumulation. This enables a person to defer taxes on many years of growth and still receive income on the accumulation.

U.S. Savings Bonds cannot be pledged as collateral for any loan.

Interest is calculated on a varying, market-related rate. When U.S. Savings Bonds are cashed in early, during the first five years, interest is credited at a lower rate. This is similar to the "substantial penalty for early withdrawal" assessed against prematurely cashing in a Certificate of Deposit at your local bank or savings and loan.

The U.S. Treasury will not permit redemption of a Savings Bond during the first six months. The occasional exception will be made "only in extreme hardship cases."

Many people purchase U.S. Savings Bonds through a company Payroll Deduction Plan. Typically Savings Bonds purchased this way are owned solely in the employee's name.

In addition to single-name ownership (which will allow Probate at the death of that individual), there are three more types of Savings Bond ownership which will affect Probate:

1 - Or. This is permitted with only one joint owner. It merely delays Probate.

2 - Beneficiary. You are permitted to name only one Beneficiary.

3 - Trust. You can retitle ownership of U.S. Savings Bonds into a Revocable Living Trust.

This book has discussed the *"or"* designation before. This is Joint Ownership, and either party can cash in the U.S. Savings Bonds. And of course, the Savings Bonds can't be left to someone else, by your Will or by any other document. They must be cashed in and taxed at the owner's death.

Designating a Beneficiary on Series E or Series H Bonds (only) has a special *dis*advantage. That person must give written permission for you to change Beneficiary. If he or she is deceased, then you must produce a Death Certificate to make the change. Series EE and Series HH Bonds do not have this requirement. For all four series of Bonds, naming a Beneficiary is the equivalent of Payment on Death (P.O.D.)

Savings Bonds are not transferable, except to certain relatives. As long as you remain part owner, the Bonds can be retitled to *"or"* joint ownership, or to a Revocable Living Trust.

To change the title or to designate a Beneficiary, you must return the Bonds with the correct U.S. Government forms. You must enlist the aid of your commercial bank or contact the U.S. Treasury Department, Bureau of Public Debt, in Washington, D.C.

Brokerage houses and savings and loans do not handle Savings Bonds due to Federal regulations.

Chapter 14
Patents, Royalties, Copyrights

"How many a man had dated a new era in his life from the reading of a book?"

—Thoreau, *Walden, 2, Reading*

"No man but a blockhead ever wrote except for money."

—Johnson (Boswell's *Life* for 1776)

Patents can only be applied for by individuals, or coinventors, or by the organization employing them.

Royalty contracts can only be applied for by individuals, or coauthors, or by the organization employing them.

Copyrights can only be applied for by individuals or coauthors, or by the organization employing them.

Patents, Royalties and Copyrights have certain characteristics in common—at least as far as their ownership is concerned.

Retitling these types of assets in order to get them into your Revocable Living Trust is more complicated than it is for most other types of assets due to various regulations and laws. Competent assistance from attorney specialists will likely be needed. Free Federal assistance is available to help you to reduce your expenses in accomplishing this important function.

To transfer ownership of a Patent, contact the Patent Office in Washington, D.C., for assistance. You can request free booklets which can assist you. For Patents, you should obtain the assistance of an experienced Patent Attorney. In addition, you should do some studying on your own first, however, as that will mean you'll require less of the Patent Attorney's expensive time. After all, attorneys usually charge by the hour because time is their only inventory. The complexity of Patent laws and regulations means that these legal specialists charge dearly for their time.

For Royalty Contracts and Copyrights you may be able to handle most of the paperwork yourself. Contact the Government Printing Office in Washington, D.C., for free assistance. Or, again, consider seeking the assistance of an attorney specializing in these areas. It still makes sense to learn something about this area *before* meeting with such attorneys in order to assist you to reduce your legal expenses.

Most estate planners recommend that your Patents, Royalty Contracts and Copyrights be titled in the name of your Revocable Living Trust in order to keep them out of Probate.

There are those who recommend establishing a separate Trust for this purpose. It really isn't necessary to do so. Remember, such retitled assets *will* avoid Probate, in a Revocable Living Trust or in a special Trust.

REREGISTRATION AT DEATH

In order to re-register a Patent, Royalty Contract or Copyright at death, your Successor Trustee needs the following:

1 - A copy of your Trust,
2 - A letter of instruction to re-register, and
3 - An "original" copy of your Death Certificate.

DURATION

Patents, Royalty Contracts and Copyrights each have different "Durations" or "Lives."

Duration of a Patent is 17 years.

Duration of a Royalty Contract is stated in the Royalty Contract itself, and is determined through negotiation. The Duration will vary from contract to contract.

Duration of a Copyright is 50 years *after the death of the author*. Make sure that the Federal Copyright Office accurately records ownership of your Copyrights by your Revocable Living Trust. This is especially important because the "Life" of a Copyright is a long one.

Chapter 15
Safe Deposit Boxes

"Safe is the word."

—John Kelly, *Scottish Proverbs (1721)*

"If it took six days to create the world, why should it take four weeks to get a loan?"

—Bank Leumi Trust Co. of NY, Advertisement

Safe Deposit Boxes are used by many people to hold jewelry and other valuables, both registered and unregistered (not titled) securities, and other important papers, such as deeds, contracts and insurance policies. You therefore should think of the contents of your Safe Deposit Box as assets.

Assuming you do not want the contents of your Safe Deposit Box to go through Probate, you should not have the box owned solely in your own name. Various forms of ownership of bank assets were discussed in Chapter 8. They all apply to Safe Deposit Boxes too.

You can own the Safe Deposit Box and name a Deputy. The Deputy is the person who has legal power of attorney which permits access to your Safe Deposit Box *as long as you are alive*. The power of attorney form is made available by the bank, typically on its Safe Deposit Box rental agreement.

Access by the Deputy is cancelled at your death. And if the owner dies, the contents of the Safe Deposit Box must go through Probate unless titled in the name of a Revocable Living Trust. A Deputy is neither a co-owner nor a Trustee.

If a Safe Deposit Box is sealed at the owner's death, a court order will be required to open it. There may be substantial delays involved. These delays vary from state to state.

A Safe Deposit Box *may* be sealed even if there is a surviving joint owner; a few states will seal one even if it's owned in the name of a Revocable Living Trust. This usually is done at the instruction of the state inheritance tax department.

These rules vary by state; within each state, there may be variations from bank to bank. The best person to discuss this with is the person in charge of *your* bank's Safe Deposit Box Department.

The general rule of thumb for your Safe Deposit Box should be the same as on all assets. It should not be owned in one name only, unless you use the "In Trust For" designation.

Remember, if you are using joint ownership ("or"), the other person owns the contents too. There may be income tax, state inheritance tax or Federal gift tax implications. Before putting another's name on assets (other than your spouse), be sure to discuss the full ramifications with your legal or tax adviser.

If the contents of your Safe Deposit Box have their own legal title (such as securities certificates), ownership is determined by that title and not by ownership of the Safe Deposit Box. Therefore, if you own the assets in the name of a Revocable Living Trust, those assets are in the Trust, irrespective of the title on the Safe Deposit Box. But it would be wisest to have the Safe Deposit Box owned by the Trust in order to provide greater access to the Box and all its contents.

If a Revocable Living Trust is the title on your Safe Deposit Box, only the Trustee(s) can have access to its contents. If you're incapacitated, your Successor Trustee would be permitted access to the Box with written statements from at least two doctors. This requirement varies by state.

Burial instructions and related documents are best *not* left in the Safe Deposit Box. If your Box were sealed, even a few days' delay could be too late for your instructions to be followed.

Counseling on prepayment and preplanning of your funeral is readily available. Discuss it with your funeral home or with a non-profit Funeral Society or Memorial Society.

Chapter 16
Small Businesses

"And that ye study to be quiet, and to do your own business."
—New Testament, *I Thessalonians IV, 11*

"Seest thou a man diligent in his business? He shall stand before kings; he shall not stand before mean men."
—Old Testament, *Proverbs, XXII, 29*

This chapter discusses various forms of ownership of small businesses — "C" Corporations, "S" Corporations, Sole Proprietorships, Partnerships and Domestic Business Trusts (Massachusetts Trusts). Ownership of a limited partnership for the purpose of this discussion appears in Chapter 10.

"C" CORPORATIONS

A "C" Corporation is a "general" corporation. It is a legal entity and pays income taxes. It can sign contracts; in a sense, it is a legal person. Unlike a "natural" person, a "C" Corporation is owned by its stockholder(s).

Evidence of legal ownership is the stock certificate. Publicly traded corporations are discussed in Chapter 10. What follows concerns privately held corporations.

One feature of both "C" and "S" Corporations is that liability of the stockholder is limited to the investment. In other words, creditors of the corporation cannot hold the stockholder personally responsible for corporate debt unless the stockholder makes himself personally responsible. A stockholder could co-sign a note, for instance.

"S" CORPORATIONS

An "S" Corporation is a corporation that's *not* taxed as an entity. Instead, its individual stockholder(s) get taxed individually. In this regard it is much like a Partnership. It, too, issues stock certificates as evidence of ownership.

The pros and cons of single and joint ownership have been examined. Like real estate, stocks held jointly cannot be *"or."* They must be *"and."*

No matter what size the corporation, or whether it's a "C" Corporation or an "S" Corporation, if the stock certificate has only one person's name on it, the death of that one person causes the certificate to become a one-way ticket to Probate.

SOLE PROPRIETORSHIPS AND PARTNERSHIPS

Many businesses are not incorporated. Incorporating a business entails expenses and paperwork. The only way your Sole Proprietorship (one owner) or interest in a Partnership (more than one owner) avoids Probate is when it's owned by a Trust. Joint ownership merely *delays* Probate.

Many businesses own assets for which no legal title exists. Three examples of such assets which come to mind are inventory, equipment and good will.

If your Sole Proprietorship is in your Trust, be sure to have your Trust appear as the purchaser on purchase orders and invoices. This will help erase doubt as to ownership of inventory and equipment.

For a Partnership, have the Partnership be the purchaser. You own only a partial interest, like one-half or 40 percent of a Partnership. Transfer your Partnership interest into your Trust by using an Affidavit of Assets.

Since typically no legal title for the Sole Proprietorship

or Partnership exists, how can you transfer that business to your Trust?

There are a couple of ways.

You could establish a separate Trust, just for your Sole Proprietorship.

You could retitle your Sole Proprietorship something like this:

Johnson Bookstore
Owned by B. L. Johnson TTEE
UTD 12/28/89
or
B.L. Johnson TTEE
DBA Johnson Bookstore
UTD 12/28/89
(DBA means Doing Business As)

Or you could simply show the Sole Proprietorship on your Affidavit of Assets and on all lists of assets you subsequently make. An Affidavit of Assets is a document prepared with your Revocable Living Trust. It lists the assets, including your business interest, which you intend to transfer into your Revocable Living Trust. This last method can apply to Partnerships; the others won't.

DOMESTIC BUSINESS TRUST

The *Domestic Business Trust* (also called the *Massachusetts Trust*) is a legal entity, similar to a corporation, that was originated to limit liability to business owners. It is the only business structure that avoids Probate and reduces estate taxes by its very nature. This structure is a little-used but increasingly popular one.

With this form of ownership, you do not need to retitle

to avoid Probate or reduce estate taxes.

SPECIAL DANGER TO SMALL BUSINESSES

There's a special danger to small businesses when they go through Probate. This danger involves the *day-to-day continuation* of the business as a going concern.

Probate will delay and possibly confuse the normal business decision-making process.

Business competitors will be aware of confidential information which they ordinarily would not have, making it easier for them to compete.

Potential customers may be reluctant to purchase additional goods or services from a business going through Probate because of concerns, valid concerns, about the ability of a business in Probate to deliver on promises on a timely basis.

Other customers will not offer to pay top price for goods and services because they assume that there's a sense of desperation about a business going through Probate.

These problems can become so severe that Probate has become a major threat to the viability of the small business and the family farm in this nation.

To illustrate the extent of this danger, there's a true story about the owner of an insurance agency who examined the Probate records of a competitor's agency. He copied the entire client list and began contacting them immediately. This severely damaged the competitor, thereby lowering its sale price. That significantly reduced what the heirs eventually received.

Simply put, the Revocable Living Trust avoids all of these problems.

Chapter 17
Motor Vehicles, Boats, Aircraft

"From going to and fro in the earth, and from walking up and down in it."

—Old Testament, *Job, I, 7*

"Ay, now I am in Arden; the more fool I; when I was at home, I was in a better place; but travellers must be content."

—Shakespeare, *As You Like It, II,4*

"Roll on, thou deep and dark-blue ocean, roll!"

—Bryon, *Childe Harold, IV*

This chapter will examine "ordinary" cars and trucks, boats, and privately-owned aircraft.

The stationary "mobile home" is usually considered real estate, especially if you own the land on which it stands. See the discussion of real estate in Chapter 9. You may want to review this with your state Department of Motor Vehicles. To be certain, use a Bill of Sale in order to transfer your mobile home to your Trust.

A "collector's car," such as a 50-year-old good-as-new antique, is for these purposes more like a coin collection (with wheels) than like the usual motor vehicle which gets used for a few years and then sold. You should consider it to be Personal Property rather than the typical automobile.

AVOID JOINT OWNERSHIP

Except for husband and wife, *do not own vehicles in Joint Tenancy*. If any type of lawsuit occurs, such as the result of an accident, *all owners can be held liable.*

Especially for motor vehicles, lawsuits are so common, and appear so large, this bears further discussion. Let's look at an example.

Ron and Sandra Teller are concerned about Probate, so they add their son's name (Willie) to the title. They know that if they die, Willie will own the car and will avoid the costs, delays and publicity of Probate. And as far as that goes, they are correct.

But son Willie is involved in an accident one day while driving Ron and Sandra's car.

The lawyer for the other side sues Willie and *all owners* of the car, thereby tying up all his parents' assets.

As you probably know, such lawsuits are quite common. Don't let this happen to you. Don't own vehicles in Joint Tenancy except husbands and wives.

In some states vehicles are exempt from Probate. Check with your legal adviser or your state Department of Motor Vehicles.

Furthermore, each state has a minimum size estate below which an estate usually escapes Probate anyway.

There are differences of opinion among estate planners regarding motor vehicles being transferred into a Revocable Living Trust. However, it can be done and they will avoid Probate.

In fact, in some locations it creates extra paperwork to sell or trade a car titled in a Revocable Living Trust.

If you determine that you want your motor vehicles in your Trust, contact your state Motor Vehicle Bureau for instructions and forms. Then, when you buy your next vehicle, do so in the name of your Trust. Be sure to follow your state's instructions carefully.

If your Revocable Living Trust has Co-trustees, *other than husband and wife,* be sure to consult with an attorney specializing in Trusts before placing motor vehicles in your Trust. *Co-trustees may be held personally liable* in some jurisdictions in case of lawsuit.

What is discussed about motor vehicles in this chapter applies generally to privately-owned aircraft and boats too. If you're concerned about exactly how this applies to your particular situation, contact the appropriate department of your state government or seek a legal specialist.

Use a Bill of Sale to transfer "rolling stock" into your Revocable Living Trust.

Chapter 18
Jewelry, Furs and Other Personal Property

"Is it not lawful for me to do what I will with mine own?"
—New Testament, *Matthew, XX, 15*

"A diamond is forever."
—De Beers, advertisement

"An ill-favored thing, sir, but mine own."
—Shakespeare, *As You Like It, V, 4*

This chapter concentrates on Personal Property, most of which has no title or other evidence of ownership.

These items include jewelry, furs, antique furniture and antique automobiles, stamp and coin collections, electronic equipment, livestock, tools, *objets d'art*, and so forth.

This category of asset has two different forms of significance for people. Both should be taken into consideration in estate planning.

First is *financial value*. And while not everyone has an original Rembrandt or Picasso on the wall, for many families Personal Property represents a very significant portion of their estates.

Second is *sentimental value*. Perhaps there is a necklace intended for your niece, or a stamp collection intended for your son, or a coin collection intended for your favorite charity. The asset itself may have insignificant *financial* value, but very significant *sentimental* value. You want specific items of your Personal Property to go to specific persons or organizations.

Without proper planning regarding asset disposition, your best intentions may not be realized. The choice is yours.

In some states, some of these assets may be subject to state inheritance tax. Contact your state Finance Department or Tax Department for details. Remember, inheritance tax and Probate are two different topics, and the Revocable Living Trust will keep your Personal Property out of Probate. It will not avoid inheritance tax.

After you establish your Trust, you can create a substitute for legal titles. When you purchase an expensive item, you should have the invoice or Bill of Sale show your Revocable Living Trust as the purchaser, instead of using your own name.

For Personal Property which you currently own, you must use a different method to accomplish transferring the assets into your Revocable Living Trust.

You should list such important *individual* items on your Affidavit of Assets and on all Schedules of Assets. Also, list "Household Furnishings" or "Farm Machinery and Equipment" or "Tools" or "Livestock" or any other accurate general category to describe the Personal Property, and the address where it's located, on the Affidavit of Assets and on all Schedules of Assets.

From time to time, you may wish to have certain items of Personal Property appraised. If so, have this done in the name of your Trust. This also will substantiate your Revocable Living Trust as owner of such untitled assets.

Some people go so far as to create a separate Revocable Living Trust just for their Personal Property. This is not the most efficient method. It certainly isn't the cheapest method.

If there are specific items of personal or other property

you wish to leave to specific individuals, you can do so by means of your Revocable Living Trust. Your Revocable Living Trust is designed for you, so if you desire special provisions to provide for certain personal items to go to certain individuals or organizations, you can have those special provisions built into your Revocable Living Trust. And those assets will avoid Probate too, of course.

Chapter 19
Retitling Revisited

"He said true things, but called them by wrong names."
—Robert Browning, *Bishop Blougram's Apology*

This book repeatedly emphasizes the vital concept of *retitling*. Some of your financial, tax, legal and estate planning advisers may make precisely the same emphasis. After all, when somebody buys or sells titled assets, retitling those assets is an essential ingredient in completing such ordinary, everyday transactions.

And so it is with the Revocable Living Trust. Retitling assets is an essential ingredient in completing this ordinary, everyday transaction too.

You should enlist the aid of various advisers to ease the way for you in getting this important task accomplished. Advisers will be discussed in greater detail later on.

It bears repeating: *If you're not going to retitle your assets, don't establish a Revocable Living Trust*. It would be a wasted effort. If your assets aren't transferred into your Trust, they won't avoid Probate. And they won't avoid Conservatorships either.

Chapter 20
Powers of Attorney

"Let George do it."
—Anonymous

The purpose of a Power of Attorney is to give somebody the legal capacity to act for you. There are different types of Powers of Attorney, three of which will be reviewed in this chapter:

1 - Limited Power of Attorney
2 - Simple Power of Attorney
3 - Durable Power of Attorney

Note: All Powers of Attorney are voided by your death.

LIMITED POWER OF ATTORNEY

A Limited Power of Attorney has limited capability. Typically it's limited to only one, or to a very small number of functions.

Remember that signature card you and your spouse or other person signed at the bank? The one that enabled you to put "or" on your joint account? That had a Limited Power of Attorney built into it. It legally enabled *either* of you to take action in the account. But since it only affects one function, such as checkwriting, it's a *Limited* Power of Attorney.

SIMPLE POWER OF ATTORNEY

That same Limited Power of Attorney on the bank signature card is also a *Simple* Power of Attorney. That doesn't necessarily mean it's easy to read and understand. It means that it's cancelled at whichever comes first: death or incapacity.

DURABLE POWER OF ATTORNEY

A Durable Power of Attorney goes through incapacity and ends at death. This is an important document and works well in connection with a Revocable Living Trust.

The Durable Power of Attorney has a special purpose. Sometimes a person becomes incapacitated because of injury or illness and that person could be laid up for a long period of time. If another person must step in to take over the orderly handling of financial and legal affairs, a Probate Court (in some jurisdictions, a Magistrate's Court) may have to create a Conservatorship or Guardianship in order to establish the legal responsibility for doing so. The court then would appoint someone, typically an attorney, to act for the incapacitated person, for a fee. And that fee is ongoing, for the entire duration of incapacity.

You can avoid this if you take action to appoint someone to act for you while you still are able to do so. This Durable Power of Attorney is the document you use to do that.

There are a few jurisdictions in which a Durable Power of Attorney is nullified if you are declared legally incompetent. If your medical and other bills are being paid, however, usually nobody will force your family to have you declared incompetent.

However, the Durable Power of Attorney gives an enormous degree of authority to someone. Grant it *only* to someone you trust implicitly.

Typically husbands and wives grant Durable Power of

Attorney to each other and then to their Successor Trustee. A single person typically grants it to his or her Successor Trustee. Of course, you can have a Limited Durable Power of Attorney.

For the duration of your incapacity, your affairs can legally be handled by your designated attorney. When you return to health and capacity, you can take back the reins, thereby regaining control of your financial and legal affairs.

Should you die without recovering, the Durable Power of Attorney would be terminated.

A Durable Power of Attorney used with a Will typically is a general, or unlimited, Power of Attorney. Many estate planners believe this allows the Attorney-in-Fact too much latitude.

And potentially it's dangerous if the person you've appointed dies or becomes incapacitated.

In any case, used with a Will, a Durable Power of Attorney won't avoid Probate in the event of your death. And it may not avoid a Conservatorship either.

It's important that you exercise extreme caution as to whom you appoint to handle these matters. If you lack *complete* confidence in the person you've selected, then *do not* authorize that person.

Chapter 21
Pour-Over Will

"Let's choose executors and talk of wills."
—Shakespeare, *Richard II, Act III, 2*

"The first thing we do, let's kill all the lawyers."
—Shakespeare, *Henry VI, Part II, Act IV, 2*

After all that's been said about Wills, after all that's been said about Probate, after all that's been said about the legal fees involved with Wills, *you may still need a Will...a Pour-Over Will.*

THE POUR-OVER WILL

You'll need a Pour-Over Will, which is a special form of "Last Will and Testament." This Will also must go through Probate. But a Pour-Over Will may be needed in conjunction with your Revocable Living Trust.

The Pour-Over Will is a special type of Will, which could become necessary even if assets are correctly retitled to avoid Probate. Without it, distribution of some of your assets may become unnecessarily complicated after your death.

Let's say that checks were issued just before the Grantors died, or even after their deaths. Those checks might be refund checks or checks for various debts owed.

Other instances might include an inheritance, an insurance settlement or lottery payments, any of which could be quite sizable.

The Pour-Over Will is a properly signed, witnessed and notarized legal document. As such, it provides for the distribution of assets not in the Revocable Living Trust.

These particular assets may go through Probate. In fact, they will go through Probate if they are of sufficient size. They then will go to the named Beneficiaries of the Trust.

The purpose of the Pour-Over Will is to act as a "catch-all" or safety net for those assets not in the Trust. There might even be some assets that did not get retitled, either through error or because the Grantors died before they could get it all done.

The Pour-Over Will leaves assets to a person as a Trustee for a Revocable Living Trust *to insert into the Trust.* It is the magnet which attracts all the loose iron filings (assets) and attracts them to the Trust. It "pours them over" into the Trust.

In some states, the term "Personal Representative" is used instead of "Executor" or "Executrix." The function is essentially the same, no matter which title is used.

As with any other Will, the Pour-Over Will can be contested and is subject to the usual delays, expenses and publicity of any other Will. But that applies only to those assets which were not retitled previously and thereby inserted into your Trust.

Meanwhile, your other Trust assets will have been distributed according to your stated wishes.

Chapter 22
The Living Will

"To every thing there is a season, and a time to every purpose under the heaven: a time to be born, and a time to die..."

—Old Testament, *Eccleslastes, III, 1-8*

Prolonged medical care and its resulting bills represent a significant threat to the ability to pass on the full value of an estate. There are those who speak of "the right to die" of a person whose life is extended only by a respirator or other artificial device when there is no reasonable medical hope of recovery. Permitting earlier death with dignity also can save the surviving family members and friends additional periods of worry and grief.

The legal document which enables a person to indicate his or her wishes in this matter is *The Living Will*. Many people, when having their Revocable Living Trusts prepared, have a Living Will prepared, too. It is a simple matter to take care of.

There are many court decisions about this sensitive matter, including the Nancy Cruzan Right-To-Die U.S. Supreme Court Case decided in the middle of 1990. In that case, the U.S. Supreme Court said that "clear and convincing" evidence of a person's desires would be the deciding factor. A properly filled out, witnessed and notarized Living Will provides that evidence.

As of this writing, nine states lack Living Will laws: Massachusetts, Michigan, Nebraska, New Jersey, New York, Ohio, Pennsylvania, Rhode Island and South Dakota. Legislation is pending in all of these states but South Dakota.

Should you be in a coma, your Living Will "clearly and convincingly" expressing your desires is essential.

In several states, the Living Will must be notarized as well as witnessed. It would be best, therefore, to have yours witnessed by two people and notarized, just to be sure.

Also, it's your responsibility to *provide copies* of your Living Will to all the appropriate parties, such as family members, physicians, clergy and friends. Be sure to speak to each such individual about this important matter, and ask your physician to make your Living Will part of your permanent medical records.

Some states have invalidated the Living Will for pregnant patients.

Your local Bar Association probably can assist you if your lawyer is unable to do so. It is not necessary to have a Revocable Living Trust in order to have a Living Will.

A comprehensive model Living Will was prepared in 1989 by a joint effort of the Midwest Bioethics Center and the Kansas City Metropolitan Bar Association.

You can contact either of these organizations for more information and a copy of their version of the comprehensive Living Will at these addresses or phone numbers:

The Midwest Bioethics Center
410 Archibald St., Suite 106
Kansas City, MO 64111
(816) 756-1735

The Kansas City Metropolitan Bar Association
1125 Grand Ave., Suite 400
Kansas City, MO 64106
(816) 474-0837

In addition, the Kansas City Metropolitan Bar Association has a recording on Living Wills available 24 hours daily at (816) 474-4100, touch-tone extension 151.

Alternatively, you can obtain additional information and appropriate documents relating to *your* state by sending a stamped, self-addressed envelope to:

The Society for the Right to Die
250 W. 57th Street
New York, NY 10107
(212) 246-6973

Chapter 23
Minor Children

"Train up a child in the way he should go; and when he is old, he will not depart from it."

—Old Testament, *Proverbs, XXII, 6*

"Out of the mouth of babes and sucklings hast thou ordained strength."

—Old Testament, *Psalms, VIII,2*

"A child should always say what's true and speak when he is spoken to, and behave mannerly at table; at least as far as he is able."

—R. L. Stevenson, *The Whole Duty of Children*

Minor children cannot own or receive title to assets legally. In this sense, an incompetent adult is treated much like a minor child.

If a person dies intestate (without a Will) and owned assets in a single name only, then generally those assets will be passed 50 percent to the spouse and 50 percent to be equally divided among the children. Some states have different rules.

If some or all of the children are minors, problems will begin.

If a person leaves assets in a Will to minors and dies, problems also will begin.

What kind of problems? Have you ever tried to open an account in a minor's name at a bank, brokerage house, or other financial institution? The institution told you that an adult was needed as Custodian for the account, under the Uniform Gifts to Minors Act (UGMA). More recently, this would have been under the Uniform Transfer to Minors Act (UTMA), which is the replacement law.

You would have used the minor's Social Security

number as a Tax Identification Number for the account, but an adult Custodian was required, until the child reaches the age of majority. The age of majority varies by state from 18 to 21.

And that's the key. A *Custodian* is needed to manage and administer the financial assets of minors.

A *Guardian* is needed to care for the children themselves. The Guardian has to keep them at their homework, to say "No" to just one more cookie, and so forth.

If you don't make proper provisions for this possibility, then someone will be appointed by the court. And the Custodian and Guardian may not be the same person!

Think of the delays and expenses then!

Let's say little Sally wants to take acting lessons. The Guardian goes to his lawyer, who goes to court, which contacts the Custodian's lawyer, who contacts the Custodian, with this request. And while we still don't know the decision, there are expenses for each step.

It's true that the Custodian and Guardian can be the same person, but courts frequently appoint different people.

But you don't have to leave it to a court. You can make your own decision. Or you can let Murphy's Law take effect.

You can use a Will to name Guardians and Custodians. It's best to do this with a Pour-Over Will in conjunction with a Revocable Living Trust. There is some variation by state; check locally as to the proper legal method of naming Guardians and Custodians.

The Pour-Over Will will catch miscellaneous assets and place them in the Trust with a duly appointed Custodian for your minor children.

Please remember, you can *appoint* a Custodian, but can only *indicate your preferences* for Guardian. A court makes the final determination of Guardian, but your indicated preference is always given primary consideration.

If you establish a Revocable Living Trust, you can provide for management of the assets. That's the job of the Trustee, who might originally have been the Successor Trustee.

A Guardianship gives minor children control of assets as soon as they reach the age of majority. Is that what you want?

Some Wills, duly constructed by lawyers, give assets to minors. This leads to Guardianships. That might be acceptable to attorneys who collect fees, but there's a better way.

Create a Revocable Living Trust and indicate Custodians and Guardians. Make your choices known. And make them take effect.

Chapter 24
Conservatorships: The Story of Groucho Marx

"The end and the reward of toil is rest."
—James Beattie, *The Minstrel, Book II*

"To none will we sell, to none deny or delay, right or justice."
—*Magna Carta (1215), Clause 40*

"We do not count a man's years, until he has nothing else to count."
—Emerson, *Society and Solitude*

When an adult is incapacitated to the extent that he or she cannot understand or make decisions, then a Conservatorship (in some jurisdictions, a Guardianship) must be established. In turn, this breaks down into two functions.

First, the Custodian is the person who manages money and other assets, under court supervision.

Second, the Guardian cares for the person; this is similar to a Guardian for a minor child.

It is not necessary for both Conservator and Guardian to be the same person.

A Conservatorship is a cumbersome, expensive process...and an unnecessary process as well.

How expensive can it be? Well, the Guardian will incur attorney's fees, as will the Custodian, for almost every financial action taken. Accounting fees may also be a factor. And continuing Probate or Magistrate Court costs will be a factor, too.

Keep in mind, a Conservatorship could continue for years. Also remember that it's the estate which is paying for all the costs. And all the costs can be avoided *completely*.

"The theory sounds interesting," you may say, "but it

can't happen to me." That's the voice of the typical American, the voice of the person who plans for death, but not for severe disability. So, as promised, what follows is the Groucho Marx story. You might have read about or heard about it.

GROUCHO

Groucho Marx—sarcastic Groucho, Groucho the punster, Groucho who made America laugh—was extremely ill for more than three years before he died. During the last three years of his life, Groucho was repeatedly wheeled into and out of court. And all America, with the help of newspapers and television, watched as this sorry spectacle unfolded.

Ms. Erin Fleming was Groucho's constant companion who lived with him in his later years. In 1974 she went to Probate Court in order to have him declared incompetent. All 50 states permit a relative or "friend" of someone to go to court in order to petition to have that person judged incompetent. If that person is determined by the court to be incompetent, then he or she is placed under the supervision of the court. In 1974, California, of course, was no exception.

After due process, Groucho was in fact found to be mentally incapacitated and incompetent to handle his affairs.

During the court proceedings, Ms. Fleming requested that she be declared both Groucho's Guardian and Groucho's Custodian. This would put her in control both of the man and his money. Groucho's family objected strenuously.

The court finally named her Groucho's Guardian, and *joint* Custodian of Groucho's money along with the Bank of America.

While this was going on, America watched. After all, an incompetency hearing is public because it is Probate for the living. Furthermore, all the information, documents and court records are open to the public. If you'd like to review this case in detail, the next time you're in Santa Monica, California, visit the county courthouse, Probate Court Division.

Ms. Fleming was only partially successful. Three years later, she was back in court. This time, she requested that she be named *sole Custodian,* over the protests of the Bank of America and Groucho's relatives.

Groucho's family actively entered the case, siding with the Bank opposing Ms. Fleming. They indicated that Ms. Fleming was greedy and selfish and was mean to Groucho.

So the Bank and the family went to court to have Ms. Fleming removed as joint Custodian and to have family members be allowed to take care of Groucho and his money.

The second set of hearings was more of a circus than the first series. The hearings dragged on for months.

Several witnesses came to testify: housekeepers, celebrities, delivery people. All came for their day in court before the cameras.

It seemed as if each day brought a spicy new allegation. There was mention of sexual favors for pay, drugs, various murder plots; all were displayed for the vicarious pleasures of the American public.

It appeared that Groucho's feelings and emotions were of no importance. His dignity was trampled upon. Every day Groucho was wheeled into and out of court, sometimes in tears, often withdrawn. After all, he and his actions were under a microscope, the center of attention in a circus.

And it didn't matter who won in court, as it became increasingly obvious that Groucho was to be the loser.

About five months after this Probate trial and public spectacle got under way, Ms. Fleming was removed as Conservator and was replaced as Guardian by Groucho's grandson.

Five days later, Groucho died.

Could this happen to you? We certainly hope not. And it won't, if you make appropriate plans.

The Revocable Living Trust, with the associated documents which are discussed in this book, will protect you and your family from concerns about Conservatorship and Probate.

Chapter 25
Advanced Trust Strategies
Malpractice/Liability Trusts and Irrevocable Complex Trusts

"I never think of the future. It comes soon enough."
—Albert Einstein, December 1930 Interview

The Revocable Living Trust is a basic estate planning strategy. You might consider the A-B or His-and-Hers Trust as an intermediate strategy because that concept not only avoids Probate but reduces estate taxes, too.

Chapter 6 discussed the A-B Trust and the Irrevocable Life Insurance Trust.

This chapter looks at more advanced strategies.

We live in a litigious society. It seems as if people sue for anything. And they try to sue for everything you have.

An advanced strategy, therefore, will allow for protection against the possibility of lawsuits taking all your assets. An advanced strategy also will minimize the cost of defending against litigation, as well as avoiding Probate and reducing estate taxes.

Incidentally, if you were to use one of the following techniques with your personally-owned assets such as your home, stocks and bonds, checking and savings accounts and so on, *those assets could be protected from being devoured automatically by nursing home or other long-term health care costs*. You may be aware of this potential danger.

This chapter examines how this strategy works in professional malpractice and product liability situations.

THE MALPRACTICE/LIABILITY TRUST

The Malpractice/Liability Trust is a special form of Trust. Originally it was designed to limit potential liability in lawsuits. It often has additional benefits which are beyond the scope of this book.

Let's examine an example of how this Trust works in limiting a medical doctor's malpractice insurance costs. It will work for *any* professional malpractice and similarly for product liability by business owners as well.

Doctor Doolittle, M.D., is a well-known obstetrician. The hospital with which he's associated requires a minimum of $1 million in malpractice insurance. Dr. Doolittle feels that this isn't enough, as his estate is worth about *$3 million*. At his own expense, he buys more than the required minimum.

In addition, he's concerned about the cost of "the tail," which means that he is liable for malpractice lawsuits after he's retired, for the rest of his life. Furthermore, *his estate may be liable for up to 14 years after his death*.

The doctor doesn't know the cost of "the tail" because it might be a lump sum premium due at the time of his retirement, or it might be included in his annual premium. Either way, the cost is substantial. Furthermore, if his wife and children outlive him, for 14 years after his death their assets (his estate) will remain potentially at risk.

He does know that the cost of this year's malpractice insurance premium is $95,000, up from last year. But he knows that his coverage should suffice to protect his estate, unless there's an enormous settlement. And that worries him. It worries him to the point where he's considering early retirement.

Then Dr. Doolittle hears of the Malpractice/Liability Trust. It enables him to reduce the cost of his malpractice insurance premium by about one-half, which means he doesn't need to raise his rates as he thought he'd have to do. And that's good news for his patients.

Let's look at how this works. To simplify the example, let's assume that Dr. Doolittle is a sole practitioner. This also would work with a group practice or a hospital, or for corporate or partnership product liability in the case of a manufacturer.

Dr. Doolittle could create a single Malpractice/Liability Trust, but instead chooses to "compartmentalize" in order to further reduce his exposure to liability. He knows that his "P.C." (Professional Corporation) does not protect his personal assets from a malpractice suit.

By "compartmentalizing" his practice, he further limits potential damage, thereby further lowering the cost of his malpractice insurance.

Of course, he still "does business" as Dr. Doolittle, P.C. But he isolates his clinic in one Trust, his equipment in another Trust, and "leases" his employees from yet a third Trust. (See Figure 19.) He then establishes a fourth Trust for management and billing.

Let's say he gets sued for malpractice. Typically, a lawyer sues for "all you've got." But this type of Trust limits the liability only to the one Trust. Let's say, for example, there was an equipment failure. In that instance, *only the Equipment Trust can be sued*. The others, because of their "compartmentalization," are not involved. They are in effect separate people.

Even more important, Dr. Doolittle's personal assets are not at risk either. Trust #1 in Figure 19 limits the lawsuit liability to its own contents.

A manufacturer or other business can use this process too, in order to limit potential damage from a product liability lawsuit.

FIGURE 19

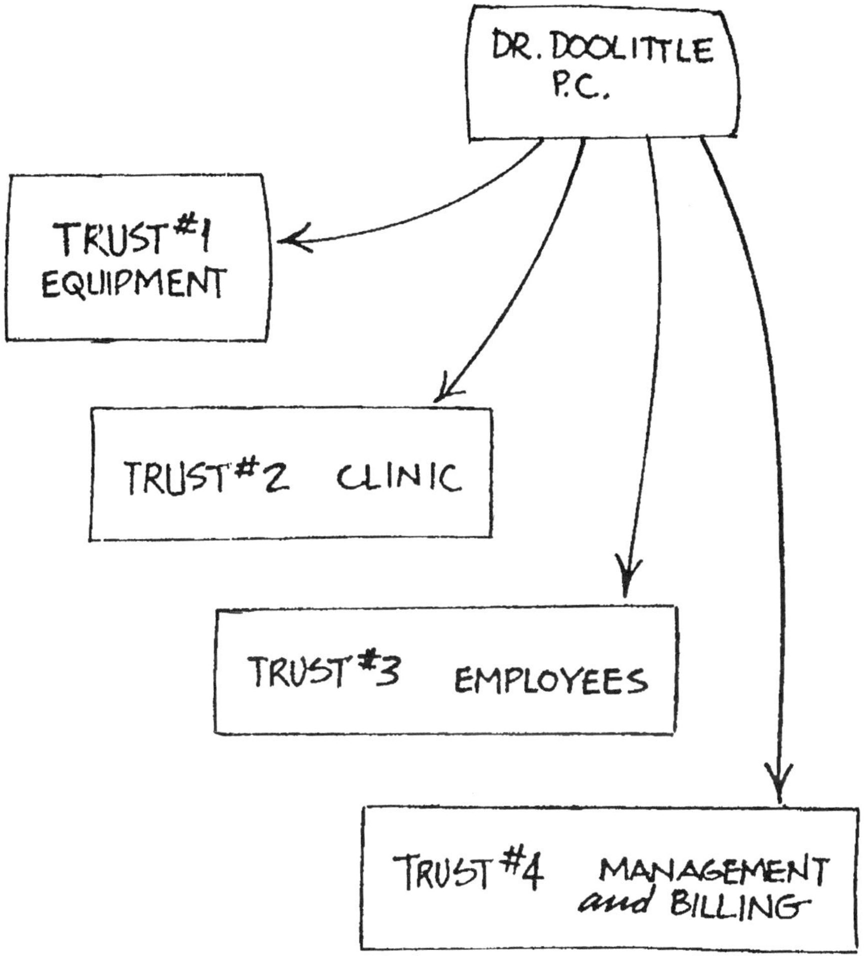

DR. DOOLITTLE
P.C.
TRUST #1
EQUIPMENT
TRUST #2 CLINIC
TRUST #3 EMPLOYEES
TRUST #4 MANAGEMENT
and BILLING

THE IRREVOCABLE COMPLEX TRUST

Some people, for various reasons, do not or cannot use the *Irrevocable Life Insurance Trust* described in Chapter 6 to solve their estate tax problem. Or they don't use that Trust to solve the problem *completely*.

In addition, such people may have additional concerns about litigation, which is not limited to professional practitioners and business owners.

It's the *Irrevocable Complex Trust* to the rescue. You can transfer assets to such a Trust in such a way that the assets will:

1 - Avoid Probate,

2 - Not be subject to estate taxes, and

3 - Not be subject to lawsuit liability.

Let's look at Tom Underwood. He has an estate worth, say, $2.5 million. His wife is deceased, and he's worried about protecting his estate from the three problems listed above.

Figure 20 shows how he proceeds.

Tom places about $550,000 of income-producing assets in his *Revocable Living Trust*, giving it a little room to grow. He gets all the income from the Trust. The balance of his estate is placed into an *Irrevocable Complex Trust*, with Tom as the manager. He gets paid for this position.

Technically, the second Trust is an artificial person. If Tom gets sued, the other "person" cannot be sued for anything that Tom may or may not have done to bring on a lawsuit. (The Trust *can* be sued for something brought on by its assets.)

Both Trusts, of course, avoid Probate.

The important advanced step is used to place assets into position so an estate tax will not be triggered. Remember, estate taxes are due nine months after death. The "artificial person" never dies! So estate taxes are never

FIGURE 20

TOM UNDERWOOD

TRANSFERS $600,000 OF ASSETS TO REVOCABLE LIVING TRUST IN HIS NAME AND PLACES THE BALANCE OF ASSETS IN AN IRREVOCABLE COMPLEX TRUST.

due.

You're going to show this idea to your attorney, who will then respond, "But I've got a gift tax problem. You're giving over $10,000 to a person, an artificial person, and your gift is a taxable event."

Your attorney is correct. *He or she* probably does have a gift tax problem because very few attorneys know how to get this done properly. *You* don't have this problem because it can be done, but must be done just so. That's one reason why it's referred to as a "Complex" Trust.

People raise the gift tax question frequently.

The gift tax "problem" *can* be solved. The three goals listed earlier *can* be attained.

There are a number of sections in the Internal Revenue Code, supported by several Federal court decisions, which indicate the continued success of this advanced strategy.

It's complicated. It works.

Furthermore, it is this tool which can save your estate from being consumed by health care costs. After all, if another person owns the assets, he or she cannot be forced legally to liquidate them for your expenses, as you would be. And the Irrevocable Complex Trust is *another person.*

As mentioned earlier, it is this technique which will protect your assets for your heirs.

Chapter 26

Where Do We Go From Here?

"Things do not change; we change."
—Thoreau, *Walden*

Where do we go from here? You've learned many things by reading this book. Our intention was to present ideas to people—ideas and information relating to the financial arena.

We're not attorneys, nor do we expect to substitute our expertise for theirs. But we *are* financial advisers, and we felt it necessary to discuss these matters from that perspective.

Do *you* need a Revocable Living Trust? Answer the following questions:

	YES	NO
1. Do I have assets worth passing on to others?	_____	_____
2. Do I care who receives such assets?	_____	_____
3. Do I care who manages these assets if I were to be incapacitated?	_____	_____
4. Do I care if my estate is distributed quickly and efficiently?	_____	_____

5. Am I concerned about the privacy of my family's finances? _____ _____

6. Are there any minors or incompetent adults about whom I am concerned? _____ _____

7. If my estate exceeds $600,000, am I concerned if the U.S. Government receives some of the assets that my heirs could receive? _____ _____

8. Do I want to be sure that certain people or organizations receive specific assets? _____ _____

If you answered "Yes" to the majority of the above questions, we urge you to consider establishing a Revocable Living Trust very seriously. And to investigate it carefully.

And if you're concerned about the possible impact of Estate Taxes on your estate, give some thought to some of the other estate planning strategies we've discussed. Visit with your legal, tax, estate planning or financial adviser. Discuss your concerns about your particular situation and investigate how these strategies might be of use to you. If they're appropriate to your situation, there's no time like the present to begin implementing these techniques.

Give some thought as to how the contents of this book might be useful to members of your family, friends, or business associates. Discuss some of these concepts with them. You'll be doing them a favor. Also, you will help clarify your own thoughts on these important matters.

And remember—this is **The Only Living Trust Book You'll Ever Need.**

Chapter 27
Getting It Done

"Everybody talks about the weather, but nobody does anything about it."

—Charles D. Warner, *Hartford Courant*

"Property has its duties as well as its rights."

—T. Drummond, *Letter to Landlords of Tipperary*

You've read this book, perhaps you've attended one or two seminars on this topic, you may have explored this with one or more of your advisers, and now you've reached the conclusion that you need a Revocable Living Trust. You've given it a lot of thought and careful consideration, and now you're ready to proceed. So how do you get it done?

There are three general methods of accomplishing this:

1. Use a do-it-yourself kit or set of papers, or
2. Use an attorney who specializes in Trusts and estate planning, or
3. Use the services of a Trust publishing and processing company.

Many people these days are establishing Revocable Living Trusts, and all three of the above methods are being used. There are pros and cons to all three of these methods, and they should be considered carefully before you proceed.

DO-IT-YOURSELF KITS

This *appears* to be the least expensive of the three methods of drawing up your Revocable Living Trust. Keep in mind, though, that you're on your own with this technique.

Usually the instructions are clearly written and easy to understand. The instructions for some, incidentally, recommend that you take the papers you've completed to an attorney for review before you execute the documents. Still others don't recommend that.

An attorney charges for time used. Paying an expert to use expensive time in order to review unfamiliar documents and recommend changes seems inefficient, to say the least.

You may even be tempted to photocopy someone else's Trust, "white out" the original names and addresses, and fill in your own information. This is potentially dangerous, as many provisions in that Revocable Living Trust may not apply to your particular situation, and others which do apply to you may be missing. Estate planners and attorneys usually advise: *Do not use another Grantor's Trust.*

While the above points out weaknesses in using a do-it-yourself kit, the main reason is that this method does not offer to answer your questions or correct your forms. Without this capability, your low-cost forms become of only limited value. You then must add expensive attorney's fees.

Approximate costs: $20-$150 PLUS legal review fees of $200-$500, for a total of $220 to $650. (A-B Trusts will cost 50 percent to 150 percent higher.)

ATTORNEYS

Generally, this is the most expensive of the three methods of obtaining your Revocable Living Trust. Please remember that most attorneys do not handle Trusts. (Most physicians do not handle brain surgery.) It is important, therefore, that if you do select an attorney, that it be one who *specializes* in this area. You don't want an attorney to *practice* on you.

If you're familiar with an attorney who does have experience in the preparation of the Revocable Living Trust, or a law firm which does so, you may want to consider pursuing this course of action with such a familiar attorney or firm.

If you're not in that position, but still want to pursue the idea of using an attorney, seek references from friends, associates, or your local Bar Association.

Interview the attorney *before* you agree to having him or her prepare your Trust. *And ask about fees.* In many cities, attorney's fees typically range from about $900 to $2,000 for a Revocable Living Trust and associated documents; an *A-B* or *His-and-Hers* Revocable Living Trust generally costs 50 percent to 150 percent more.

When you seek an attorney, consider the following:

1) If an attorney declines to meet you for a no-cost, no-obligation brief interview, *disqualify him or her* and find somebody else.

2) If a lawyer attempts to steer you toward the use of a *Testamentary Trust*, this also should be cause for *disqualification*, as the *Testamentary Trust* won't avoid Probate.

3) If an attorney tells you that your under-$600,000 estate is too small for a Revocable Living Trust, *disqualify* that lawyer. Either this attorney is trying to obtain your Probate business, or he or she doesn't know the difference between Probate and Federal Estate Taxes...and you *do* know the difference! You might even ask such an attorney to put in writing on his or her letterhead that your estate is too small for a Revocable Living Trust and that it will avoid Probate. Then, seek another lawyer after your

request is denied.

4) If an attorney declines to give you a price, or at least an *estimated* price for your Revocable Living Trust, look elsewhere. Preparation of these documents is largely a word-processing function, and an experienced Trust attorney knows approximately what the fee will be. Declining to provide you with a price should be cause for *disqualification.*

5) If an attorney does not prepare *all* the associated documents described earlier, *disqualify* him or her. (Would you buy an automobile without wheels and headlights?)

6) If an attorney will not discuss or describe *retitling,* this too should be cause for *disqualification.*

YOUR EXPERTISE

Having read this book and perhaps others, as well as performing any other research, you're now prepared to speak intelligently and knowledgeably with a Trust attorney. *Don't be intimidated.*

USE THE SERVICES OF A TRUST PUBLISHING AND PROCESSING COMPANY

This method typically is less expensive than working *directly* with an attorney and more expensive than using a do-it-yourself kit without using an attorney. If you use this method, be sure that the company is a *full-service* Trust processing company. They should have a lawyer involved; they should do the paperwork for you; they should answer your questions while your Trust is being prepared; and they should be available to answer your questions and guide you after the Trust becomes a legal entity.

A Trust publishing and processing company works with this procedure:

1) After you've paid, they'll gather information from you. This includes asset details, Beneficiaries that you've selected, how your estate is to be dispersed after your death, Successor Trustees and so forth. This can be done in person, on the phone, by mail, or by fax. An attorney will require the same information.

2) At this point, there typically will be a brief period during which you can request a refund. Once they begin preparation of documents, however, this period ceases.

3) A *first draft* of the documents will be sent to you for proofreading. Be sure to do so very carefully, looking for spelling and number errors, and any omissions by them or by you.

4) After they receive your corrected or approved documents, a final draft will be provided, ready to be signed, witnessed and notarized.

There are several Trust publishing and processing companies around the country. One such Trust publishing and processing company is:

The House of Trust
7180 W. 107th Street
Overland Park, KS 66212
(913) 648-2712

Their Trust processing department has been preparing *lawyer-reviewed* Revocable Living Trusts since 1977. They've prepared *thousands* of Revocable Living Trusts for residents of all 50 states and their Trust consultants are knowledgeable and helpful.

Another Trust publishing and processing company preparing lawyer-reviewed Revocable Living Trusts is:

Living Trusts America
33313 1st Way South
Federal Way, WA 98003
(206) 874-9608

There are many others nationwide. Costs generally are from $250 to $1000. A-B Trusts cost 50 percent to 150 percent more.

Whichever method you finally select, congratulations! You're on the road to avoiding Probate. In fact, you *can*

STOP PROBATE NOW!

Appendix I
Glossary

A-B Trust - See *His-and-Hers Trust.*

Administration - After one dies, the period during which his or her affairs are handled under the supervision of the Court. Similar to Probate.

Administrator - The person appointed by the Court to handle an administration when there was no Will-named executor. (Fem. - Administratrix.)

Affidavit of Assets - A document prepared along with a Revocable Living Trust which lists the assets you intend to transfer into your Trust.

Alternate Valuation Date - Six months after the date of death, this date may be elected by heirs to value all assets in the estate. This is an alternate selection to the actual date of death. See *Stepped-Up Basis.*

Ancillary - See *Multiple Probate.*

Attorney - A person empowered to act for another. See *Attorney-in-Fact; Lawyer.*

Attorney-in-Fact - Under a Power of Attorney, the person or agent granted the legal right to act. See *Power of Attorney.*

Backup Trustee - See *Successor Trustee.*

Basis - Capital gains are the surplus of net proceeds of a sale minus gross cost to acquire (basis). The acquisition (basis) cost may be adjusted. See *Stepped-up Basis. Capital Gains.*

Beneficiary - The person to receive or benefit from the assets and income of a Trust (or of a Life Insurance Policy, Annuity or Retirement Plan). Sometimes it also means the person to whom assets are distributed by means of a Will. In addition, it is the person for whom assets are managed in a Trust. See *Heir.*

Bequest - That property which is bequeathed or left to another person by means of a Will. See *"Devise and Bequeath."*

Bill of Sale - The document used to indicate the transfer of untitled rolling stock into a Trust.

Bond - A guarantee by an insurance company or bonding agency to repay any loss due to negligence or criminal cause by an Executor or Administrator. Many Revocable Living Trusts, with family members or friends as Trustees, specify no bond as being necessary.

Buy-Sell Agreement - An agreement among partners in or co-owners of a business which specifies the terms for buying out one's share at death. A similar agreement may be established for disability.

Capital Gains - The profits which are realized (obtained) by the sale of one or more capital assets. It is the difference between the *gross* cost to acquire (including commissions or fees) and the *net* proceeds. If this arithmetic yields a negative figure, it is then referred to as a *capital loss*. See *Basis*.

Chancery Court - This is what Probate Court is called in some jurisdictions. See *Probate Court*.

Codicil - The document which amends or supplements a Will.

Common Occurrence - An accident involving two or more people simultaneously, typically fatally. Could cause jointly owned property to go through Probate. See Chapter 2.

Community Property - Property which was acquired in the "Community Property" states by a married couple while they're married, and which doesn't include separate property, including any earnings related to that property or to the marriage.

Conservatorship - Not available in all states. This resembles a Guardianship for an incompetent person, but generally avoids the aura of incompetence. See Chapter 24.

Contest - See *Will Contest*.

Contingent Successor Trustee - The backup to the Successor Trustee, if that person cannot or will not act or function. See *Successor Trustee* and Chapter 4.

Corpus - See *Principal*.

Court Trust - A Trust which is under the continuing oversight and jurisdiction of a court, usually Probate Court or its equivalent.

Creator - See *Grantor.*

Creditor Claims - When creditors of the decedent wish to be paid from assets of the estate, they must file these documents.

Curtesy - Obsolescent term for a husband's rights. It's the mirror image of Dower. See *Dower.*

Custodian - The person or organization managing assets for minor children or incompetent adults. See Chapters 23 and 24.

Death Trust - See *Testamentary Trust.*

Deceased - See *Decedent.*

Decedent - Widely-used legal term for a person who has died; the deceased.

Deduction - An item that is permitted to be subtracted or deducted from taxable income, taxable gifts, or a taxable estate. This results in reducing taxes due. See *Unlimited Marital Deduction.*

"Devise and Bequeath" - Traditional words used in a Will to pass property to heirs. See *Bequest.*

Disability - See *Incompetence.*

Domicile - The state or county wherein the decedent lived or intended his permanent home to be; also determines the taxing and Probate jurisdictions.

Donee - The person who receives property, or to whom a Power of Appointment is given.

Donor - See *Grantor.*

Dower - Obsolescent term referring to the share of marital property automatically granted to the wife upon her husband's death in community property states. See *Community Property; Curtesy.*

Due on Sale - A clause included in many mortgage contracts which requires full payment of any remaining mortgage balance when that property is sold. Using a *Quit-Claim Deed* to transfer real estate into a Revocable Living Trust does *not* constitute a sale of that property. It's considered wise to contact your mortgage lender when you're about to make this transfer. See Chapter 9 and Appendix III.

Durable Power of Attorney - A form of Power of Attorney which lasts through disability. A *limited* Durable Power of Attorney limits the functions of the Attorney-in-Fact, to be tied closely with a Revocable Living Trust. See Chapter 20.

Escheat - If a person were to die without a Will (*Intestate*) and there are no heirs, then the assets of the estate go to the state, after all bills are paid. See *Intestate.*

Estate - The assets owned by the decedent at the time of death.

Estate Tax - The tax levied on the deceased's right to leave property to others at death. This is imposed by the Federal government and by some state governments. See Chapters 5, 6 and 25; *Inheritance Tax.*

Executor - A person whom a Will names to administer the Probate process under the supervision of the Probate Court. In some jurisdictions this person is called a Personal Representative. (Fem. - Executrix.)

Exemption - The amount below which a tax does not apply or which refers to an amount excluded from the calculation of that tax. For instance, as of this writing there is a $600,000 exemption for Federal Estate Taxes. Thus, an estate of $600,000 or less is not taxed; any amount over this exemption is subject to Federal Estate Tax.

Family Allowance - An amount allocated for the support of a spouse and children by Probate Court. The obsolete usage is "Widow's Allowance."

Fee Simple - Property ownership in a single name, with no other interest by others and no chance of losing such ownership.

Fiduciary - A person who acts in the best interest of another, under high legal and ethical standards. This includes Trustees, Executors, Guardians, and Conservators among others.

Funded Trust - A Revocable Living Trust that has had assets retitled and transferred into it in order to avoid Probate.

Gift Tax - A tax on the right of someone to make gifts to others.

Grantor - The person(s) creating the Trust, who owned the assets being retitled and transferred into the Trust to avoid Probate. Sometimes called Donor, Settlor, Trustor or Creator.

Gross Estate - The total value of all assets in an estate, ignoring outstanding liabilities such as mortgages owed. Typically, it is the value upon which Probate fees are based.

Guardian - The person or organization managing a Guardianship. See *Guardianship* and Chapter 23.

Guardianship - The administration or management of the property (and frequently of the person) of minor children or incompetent adults, under court supervision. The supervising court usually is Probate Court or its equivalent. See Chapter 23.

Heir - The person receiving assets from a Will or intestacy which has been Probated. Sometimes this term refers to the recipient of assets by means of a Trust distribution, but "Beneficiary" is a more accurate term. See *Beneficiary*.

His-and-Hers Trust - A special Revocable Living Trust, sometimes called an A-B Trust, which is used to reduce Federal Estate Tax for married couples by obtaining two exemptions, one each for husband and wife. See Chapter 5.

Incapacity - See *Incompetence*.

Incompetence - Sometimes called Disability or Incapacity. Refers to a person unable to function, to act legally, to take care of his or her own affairs. See *Conservatorship* and Chapter 24.

Inheritance Tax - A tax levied by some states on the right of heirs to inherit assets. Although it appears to be similar to an Estate Tax, and has the same effect of reducing the value of assets owned by the recipient, an inheritance tax is imposed on the *heir* and not on the estate. See *Estate Tax.*

Inter Vivos - Latin for "while living." *Inter Vivos* is frequently used to refer to a Revocable Living Trust. See *Revocable Living Trust.*

Intestacy - Referring to the condition of dying without a valid Will. See *Intestate.*

Intestate - A person who dies without having left a valid Will, or without any Will at all, is said to die *intestate.* At that time state intestacy laws will determine who is to receive assets from the estate. A Revocable Living Trust avoids intestacy, too. Intestacy does not avoid Probate.

In Trust For (I.T.F.) - Sometimes called a "Totten Trust." This designation is used on some bank accounts in an attempt to avoid Probate. See Chapter 8.

Inventory - A Probate Court listing which shows the value of all assets contained in a Probated estate. This information is a matter of public record, available to anyone upon request.

Irrevocable Trust - A Trust that cannot be amended or

revoked by its Grantor(s). In certain respects, some Irrevocable Trusts are considered to be artificial persons—just as corporations are artificial persons. See Chapters 6 and 25.

Joint-and-Mutual Will - One Will which is signed by both spouses and which arranges disposition of their assets after each death. This can lead to more than one Probate as well as to other complications. Many attorneys and estate planners strongly suggest that this type of Will should be avoided.

Joint Tenancy With Right of Survivorship (JTWROS) - Shared ownership by two or more people, with survivor(s) owning property after death of one or more owners. It delays Probate, but doesn't avoid it. See Chapter 2.

Lawyer - One whose profession is to give legal advice and assistance. See *Attorney*.

Letters Testamentary - Term used in some jurisdictions to refer to the legal document which provides the proper authority for an Executor to act for the estate of a deceased person.

Limited Power of Attorney - A Power of Attorney with limited function. When created in conjunction with a Revocable Living Trust, it typically limits functions to those related to that Trust. See Chapter 20.

Living Trust - See *Revocable Living Trust*.

Living Will - The legal document which indicates a

person's wishes regarding his or her right to die. See Chapter 22.

Magistrate's Court - In some jurisdictions, this performs the function of Probate Court.

Marital Deduction - The deduction from death taxes for all property left to the surviving spouse by decedent spouse. For Federal Estate Taxes, there is an unlimited marital deduction. See *Unlimited Marital Deduction.*

Multiple Probate - If a decedent owned real estate in more than one state, there may be a Probate process for each state in which the real estate is located. This is sometimes called "Ancillary."

Murphy's Law - Referring to uncertainty in a cynical manner, purported to be: "If something can go wrong, it will go wrong."

Myth - An invented story, which contains at least one underlying false premise. See Chapters 1, 2 and 3.

Net Estate - The total value of all assets in an estate, reduced by all liabilities (amounts owed) by the estate. Generally, the net estate is the amount subject to estate taxes, reduced by statutory exemptions.

No Contest Clause - A clause in some Wills which attempts to disinherit any person trying to attack the validity of such a Will.

Non-Court Trust - A Trust, such as a Revocable Living Trust, that is not subject to the ongoing supervision or oversight of a court.

Notice to Creditors - A notice which tells creditors of the decedent's death, allowing them to enter claims against the estate.

Partition - A court proceeding which permits a joint owner of property to create a separation or partition of ownership interests. This is frequently accomplished by means of a court-ordered auction sale, with sale proceeds divided among the owners.

Payable on Death (P.O.D.) - A commonly used method to have bank assets avoid Probate. It sometimes works. See Chapter 8.

Per Capita - The sharing of an inheritance by relatives of the decedent in equal shares, determined by the degree of their relationship to the decedent.

Per Stirpes - Latin for "by the branch." In estates, it means a deceased child's children share his or her inheritance equally.

Personal Property - Both tangible and intangible assets other than real estate. Most frequently used to describe untitled personal assets, such as jewelry, artworks, clothing, furniture, etc.

Personal Representative - *See Executor.*

Pour-Over Will - A Will that "pours over" or leaves property to an *existing* Revocable Living Trust. While it seems to work like a Testamentary Trust, it allows Probate to affect *only* those assets not retitled. See *Testamentary Trust* and Chapter 21.

Power of Attorney - A document which legally grants another person the ability to act for you. It becomes void at your death or incapacity, except that a Durable Power of Attorney lasts through incapacity up to your death. See *Durable Power of Attorney* and Chapter 20.

Preliminary Distribution - A partial distribution of an estate's assets before the estate is closed out. This sometimes is done to provide family members with funds to avoid financial hardship while the balance of the estate is being Probated.

Principal - The assets which make up a Trust. Sometimes referred to as the "Corpus."

Probate - Sometimes called administration, Probate is the process of legally validating a Will or Intestacy. It provides for the retitling of assets if no survivors are still named on their titles. It serves the purpose of transferring ownership from the deceased to the living. It is an expensive and cumbersome process which is avoided by the Revocable Living Trust.

Probate Court - A state court where Probate is processed. This includes both Living Probate (Guardianships, Conservatorships) and Death Probate (to transfer ownership of decedent's assets). In some jurisdictions, "Magistrate's Court" or "Surrogate Court" or "Chancery Court" handles the Probate function.

Public Record -Refers to the lack of privacy of the Probate process. See *Probate* and Chapter 1.

Quit-Claim Deed - Document used to transfer real estate into a Trust. See Chapter 9.

Real Property - Land (real estate) and anything which grows on it or is permanently part of it (such as buildings).

Remainder - The assets remaining in an estate for a new owner, after a temporary interest has ended. This usually occurs after the death of the person who had the interest in the estate.

Residue - That portion of the estate, *after* specific items (such as jewelry) have been given to specified individuals, which remains to be distributed, typically according to the terms of a Will or a Trust.

Retitling - The process which legally transfers *title* of property from the name(s) of the Grantor(s) to the name of a Revocable Living Trust. Without retitling assets, a Trust is unfunded and ineffective. When you establish your Revocable Living Trust, *be sure* to retitle your assets. See *Unfunded Trust* and Chapters 7 and 19 and Appendix III.

Revocable Living Trust - A Trust established during the lifetime of the Grantor(s). It instructs the Trustee(s) as to management of Trust assets, and can be amended or revoked (cancelled) at any time by the Grantor(s). Sometimes called an Inter Vivos Trust. See Chapter 4.

Revocation - The act of revoking or terminating a Trust; also, the document which revokes a Trust. Also to be used to revoke or cancel a Will.

Right of Survivorship - Refers to Joint Tenancy With Right of Survivorship (JTWROS). Surviving joint tenants automatically have rights of ownership after the death of the other joint owner(s). This *postpones* Probate—it does not avoid it. See *Joint Tenancy With Right of Survivorship* and Chapter 2.

Second to Die Policy - See *Survivorship Policy.*

Self-Proving - Some states permit a Will to contain certain clauses built in to the Notary's signature "guarantee" which eliminates the need to call witnesses to court to testify at decedent's Probate proceedings. If you are writing your own Will, investigate this carefully. Better yet, establish a Revocable Living Trust.

Settlor - See *Grantor.*

Spendthrift Clause - A Trust clause preventing a creditor from attacking a Beneficiary's interest; also applies to Life Insurance proceeds to be paid. See Chapter 12.

Stepped-Up Basis - Heir's cost basis is equal to the value of inherited assets at the date of death or, alternatively, six months later. See *Alternate Valuation Date; Basis.*

Stock-and-Bond Powers - A written authorization document separate from the actual stock or bond certificate, giving permission to transfer title of the certificate.

Successor Trustee - The manager of Trust assets who backs up the initial Trustee. Sometimes called "Backup

Trustee". See Chapter 4.

Surrogate Court - In some jurisdictions, this is Probate Court.

Survivorship Policy - A Life Insurance policy which insures a *couple* instead of an individual. It's used to offset estate taxes; proceeds aren't paid until the second spouse dies. Referred to as a "Second to Die Policy" by some. See Chapter 6.

Tenancy By The Entirety - Not available in all states; Joint Tenancy which is available for husbands and wives only, and generally used only for real estate. Delays Probate. See Chapter 2.

Tenancy in Common - Joint Tenancy which has *no* rights of survivorship. At the death of one or more owners, Probate will be necessary. Probate is neither avoided nor delayed. See Chapter 2.

Testamentary Trust - A Trust which is part of a Will and *which comes into existence after death and after Probate.* Only then are assets transferred to the Testamentary Trust. This is clearly inferior to the Revocable Living Trust. After all, why should assets be Probated when Probate can be avoided completely?

Testate - Dying and leaving a valid Trust of Will. See *Intestate.*

Testator - A person who creates and executes a Will. (Fem.- Testatrix.)

Totten Trust - See *In Trust For.*

Transfer on Death (T.O.D.) - A flawed method of avoiding Probate on certain bank accounts. See Chapter 8.

Trust - A legal written arrangement in which one or more Trustees manage assets for the benefit of one or more Beneficiaries. See Chapter 4.

Trust Processing Company - A company which specializes in the processing of Trusts, especially Revocable Living Trusts. See Chapter 27.

Trustee - The person(s) or organization managing Trust assets for the benefit of one or more Beneficiaries. See Chapter 4.

Trustor - See *Grantor.*

Undivided Interest - The partial interest owned by a Tenant in Common. Also, if a His-and-Hers Trust is established and the assets are divided between both Trust parts while husband and wife still live, those assets which can't be divided (a house, a horse, a cow, etc.) would, if divided equally, be listed as "one-half undivided interest in ____________."

Unfunded Trust - A Trust to which assets have not been transferred, or retitled. See *Retitling* and Chapters 7 and 19.

Unlimited Marital Deduction - This deduction permits spouses to transfer an unlimited amount of property to each other (while alive or after death) without any type of gift tax, income tax or estate tax implications. See *Deduction.*

Widow's Allowance - See *Family Allowance.*

Will - A document which directs Probate Court as to disposition of decedent's assets after death. It also may *recommend* Guardians for minors. See Chapter 1.

Will Contest - A legal challenge to a Will, usually made by one or more disgruntled heirs. It often is based on alleged improper execution of the Will, or lack of proper mental capacity to create the Will in the first place. It results in lengthening the Probate process. See Chapter 1.

Appendix II
Estate Value Estimation

For Probate purposes, your *gross estate* is needed, adjusted as shown below. For estate tax purposes, only your *net estate* is needed. Use the following in order to estimate both values. (A Federal Estate Tax chart appears in Chapter 5.)

ASSETS

Checking/NOW Accounts	$ ________
Savings	$ ________
Credit Union Accounts	$ ________
Money Market Funds	$ ________
CDs	$ ________
U.S. Savings Bonds	$ ________
U.S. Treasury Bonds/Notes/Bills	$ ________
Municipal Bonds	$ ________
Corporate Bonds	$ ________
GNMAs	$ ________
Other U.S. Agency Issues	$ ________
Notes Receivable	$ ________
Mortgages Owned	$ ________
Stocks	$ ________
Mutual Funds	$ ________
Limited Partnerships	$ ________
Annuities*	$ ________

IRAs/Keoghs/SEPs*	$ ________
Pension/Other Retirement Plans*	$ ________
Life Insurance* (Face value)	$ ________
Home	$ ________
Other Real Estate	$ ________
Business Interests	$ ________
Personal Property (cars, jewelry, antiques, etc.)	$ ________
Other Assets	$ ________
TOTAL ASSETS	$ ________

LIABILITIES

Home Mortgage Balance	$ ________
Home Equity Loan Balance	$ ________
Other Real Estate Loans	$ ________
Student Loans	$ ________
Car Loans	$ ________
Credit Card Balances	$ ________
Notes Payable	$ ________
Other Amounts Payable	$ ________
TOTAL LIABILITIES	$ ________

Assets	—	Liabilities	=	Net Estate
$ ________	—	$ ________	=	$ ________

***Note:** Subtract these assets from your gross estate for

Probate purposes *only*. Do *not* adjust for Federal Estate Taxes.

Life Insurance proceeds, annuities and/or retirement plan assets (including IRAs) will avoid Probate if there is at least one Beneficiary available to receive the assets at the time of your death. See Chapters 11 and 12.

Do not include in your gross or net estate valuation any accounts for which you are Custodian for a minor, such as Uniform Gifts to Minors Act (UGMA) or Uniform Transfer to Minors Act (UTMA) accounts. Also, do not include any account for which you act as Trustee. You don't own any of these accounts. Therefore, they are not in your estate and are not subject to estate taxes or Probate upon your death.

Appendix III
Retitling Made Easy

A large portion of this book has been devoted to *retitling* assets because many estate planners agree that insufficient emphasis has been given to this important topic. The *retitling* process for your Revocable Living Trust, which begins once the Trust is established, is simple and straightforward. In order to assist you in completing this vital step in avoiding Probate, this book illustrates some model letters which you can use to fund your Revocable Living Trust. Use the models *after* you speak to the proper parties.

Please remember—stockbrokerages, real estate firms, insurance companies, banks, saving and loan companies, mutual fund companies, law firms, accounting firms and others can assist you in handling this vital step quickly and efficiently. Whenever you feel it's appropriate, ask for their help.

After you've instructed an institution to make the change of ownership, make sure the institution follows your instructions *precisely* and *promptly*. Computers merely follow instructions provided by *humans*. And we humans are notoriously imperfect.

TRUST NAME

Your Revocable Living Trust will have a legal name or title that you must know in order to retitle (transfer) assets. This name will contain the Trustee(s) name(s), the name of the Trust which may or may not be the same as the name(s) of the Grantor(s), and the date the Trust was executed (signed, witnessed and notarized). For example, the Michael and Helen Hunt (under $600,000) Trust, executed August 1, 1990, would be named as follows, which may vary somewhat by state or even by institution:

> **Michael Hunt and Helen Hunt Trustees for**
> **The Michael Hunt and Helen Hunt Trust**
> **UTD * 8/1/90**

*UTD or UAD means Under Trust Dated or Under Agreement Dated. Sometimes Trustee is abbreviated: TTEE.

Again, be sure that *all* institutions change their records to show this type of listing for your Trust assets.

<u>Bank, S & L, Credit Union</u>

Dear ____________________

This is to confirm our discussion of (*date*) regarding change of title of the following account(s) to my (our) Revocable Living Trust:

Current Title	Account Type	Account #

Please change the title on each account to:

INSERT TRUST TITLE HERE

I (we) depend on you to take all the necessary steps to

accomplish this correctly and promptly. Please notify me (us) in writing when this has been accomplished.

Very truly yours,

Most of these institutions will require you to use their forms, as well as provide them with copies of your *complete* Trust. This last appears to be an invasion of your privacy—many estate planners and lawyers think this should be resisted. Some institutions will request only the title page and Trustee page, which is more reasonable. It's difficult to find any that don't require any part of your Trust—which would be best of all.

<u>Stocks, Bonds, Etc. (Account change)</u>

Dear ______________________

This it to confirm our discussion of (*date*) regarding change of title of account # (*number*), currently titled (*show current name*). Please change the title to read as follows:

INSERT TRUST TITLE HERE

I (we) depend on you to perform all the necessary steps to accomplish this correctly and promptly. Please notify me (us) in writing when this has been accomplished.

Very truly yours,

Stocks, Bonds, Etc. (When you have certificates)

Dear ____________________

On (*date*), I left security certificates with you, deposited to account # (*number*), in order to transfer title to read as follows:

INSERT TRUST TITLE HERE

I (we) depend on you to perform all the necessary steps to accomplish this correctly and promptly, and to return the retitled certificates as soon as possible, so that my (our) personal planning can be accomplished.

Very truly yours,

When the certificates are left in the account ("in street name") for your Trust, *some* firms will require a *complete copy* of your Revocable Living Trust. This appears to be an invasion of your privacy—many estate planners and lawyers think this should be resisted. Some firms request only the title page and Trustee page, which is more reasonable. Some ask you merely to sign a form, which is best of all.

If you're requesting replacement certificates (inferior to leaving securities in the account), there's no reason why a copy of your Trust is needed *for your benefit*.

Some stockbrokerages may charge a fee for this service. Be sure to ask.

Instead of having a stockbrokerage firm retitle your

certificates, you can do so yourself. Merely write directly to *each* Transfer Agent named on the security certificate. It's best to include photocopies of each certificate.

Use the following as a model:

Gentlemen:

This refers to (identify the security) certificate(s) numbered (insert certificate numbers), photocopy (photocopies) enclosed.

For estate planning purposes, I (we) want to retitle these assets into the name of my (our) Revocable Living Trust. Please send me (us) the appropriate forms and instructions.

Thank you.

Very Truly Yours,

It typically takes one to three weeks to obtain a response and an additional four to six weeks to obtain replacement certificates...if no errors are made. Using the services of a stockbrokerage firm is far superior.

Retirement Plans

To change Beneficiaries on company plans, contact your Employee Benefits or Personnel Department and ask them to help you fill out the forms.

Use the following to change the Beneficiary on your IRA, Keogh or SEP, after talking to your representative:

Dear ____________________

This is to confirm our discussion of (*date*) regarding change of Beneficiary for (*plan type-IRA, etc.*) account # (*number*).

Please change the primary Beneficiary to:

Spouse or Trust Title (See Chapter 11)

Please change Contingent Beneficiary to: **INSERT TRUST TITLE** (only if spouse is your primary Beneficiary. If your Trust is primary Beneficiary, delete reference to a Contingent Beneficiary—it's unnecessary. See Chapter 11.)

I (no *we* here) depend on you to perform all the necessary steps to accomplish this correctly and promptly. Please notify me in writing when this has been accomplished.

Very truly yours,

Almost all IRA/Keogh/SEP Custodians will require you to use their forms. Do so, following directions carefully. Ask for any help you need.

Insurance

Dear ____________________

This it to confirm our discussion of (*date*) regarding change of Beneficiary on the policy (policies) shown below. Change the following (life insurance, disability insurance) policy (policies):

Insured	Company Name	Policy Number

Please change the primary Beneficiary to:

INSERT TRUST TITLE HERE

I (we) depend on you to perform all the necessary steps to accomplish this correctly and promptly. Please notify me (us) in writing when this has been accomplished.

Very truly yours,

Some companies may require use of their own forms for Change of Beneficiary. If so, your local agent can obtain them for you. If you have no local agent, contact the company directly (there may be a local or regional office nearby).

For employer-owned policies, contact your Employee Benefits or Personnel Department. Have them help you fill out the forms.

Mortgage Lender

Transferring real estate into a Revocable Living Trust is

not a sale. Nonetheless, in order to avoid any questions or problems with your mortgage lender, call the company *before* you transfer title. This does not trigger the "Due on Sale" clause in your mortgage because you are not selling the real estate.

Explain to the person with whom you speak that you are transferring title for Estate Planning purposes. If you talk to an inexperienced person who is unfamiliar with the Revocable Living Trust, ask for an officer of the company. Be sure to follow your conversation with a letter like this:

Dear ____________________

This is to confirm our discussion of (*date*) regarding the transfer of title of my (our) property (properties) at ____ ____________________________________ to that of my (our) Revocable Living Trust.

As indicated in the discussion, this is not a sale. Rather, it is for personal estate planning purposes only.

Thank you for your cooperation.

Very truly yours,

Once your Revocable Living Trust comes into being, it is important for you to begin retitling your assets *promptly*. If you do so completely you'll find that you *do* have the power to

STOP PROBATE NOW!

Index

A

B

C

D

Q

R

S

T

U

W

Order Books for Gifts

STOP Probate NOW! The Only Living Trust Book You'll Ever Need is an excellent gift for your friends and loved ones. Ideal for birthdays, anniversaries, retirements and holidays, it makes a timely present that will be appreciated for years to come. The information in the book includes valuable answers for everyone who has serious questions about the high cost of Probate and the long court delays it involves. **Copy the order form** on this page or remove it where indicated on the left. We will mail the book first class and enclose a personalized gift card, too!

$19.95 plus $3.00 Postage and Handling for each book.
(Kansas residents add .625% sales tax)
Quantity discounts for groups and organizations
are available for 25 books and more.

Please print

Name ______________________________

Address ______________________________

City ____________________ State ____ Zip ________

Phone Bus. ____________________ Home ________________

Please Mail To:

Name ______________________________

Address ______________________________

City ____________________ State ____ Zip ________

Phone Bus. ____________________ Home ________________

Inscription on gift card ______________________________

____

❑ Check Enclosed ❑ Money Order Enclosed
(Please make payable to Trust Publishing Company)

❑ MasterCard ❑ Visa ❑ American Express

Card # ____________________ Expiration Date ____________

Cardholder's Signature ______________________________

Mail to **Trust Publishing Company**
10308 Metcalf, Suite 257 • Overland Park, KS 66212

For faster service phone **Toll Free 1-800-835-0220 Extension 284**

Order Books for Gifts

STOP Probate NOW! The Only Living Trust Book You'll Ever Need is an excellent gift for your friends and loved ones. Ideal for birthdays, anniversaries, retirements and holidays, it makes a timely present that will be appreciated for years to come. The information in the book includes valuable answers for everyone who has serious questions about the high cost of Probate and the long court delays it involves. **Copy the order form** on this page or remove it where indicated on the left. We will mail the book first class and enclose a personalized gift card, too!

$19.95 plus $3.00 Postage and Handling for each book.
(Kansas residents add .625% sales tax)
Quantity discounts for groups and organizations
are available for 25 books and more.

Please print

Name ______________________________

Address ______________________________

City ____________________ State _____ Zip ________

Phone Bus. ____________________ Home ____________

Please Mail To:

Name ______________________________

Address ______________________________

City ____________________ State _____ Zip ________

Phone Bus. ____________________ Home ____________

Inscription on gift card ______________________________

____

☐ Check Enclosed ☐ Money Order Enclosed
(Please make payable to Trust Publishing Company)

☐ MasterCard ☐ Visa ☐ American Express

Card # ____________________ Expiration Date ________

Cardholder's Signature ______________________________

Mail to **Trust Publishing Company**
10308 Metcalf, Suite 257 • Overland Park, KS 66212

For faster service phone **Toll Free 1-800-835-0220 Extension 284**

Order Books for Gifts

STOP Probate NOW! The Only Living Trust Book You'll Ever Need is an excellent gift for your friends and loved ones. Ideal for birthdays, anniversaries, retirements and holidays, it makes a timely present that will be appreciated for years to come. The information in the book includes valuable answers for everyone who has serious questions about the high cost of Probate and the long court delays it involves. **Copy the order form** on this page or remove it where indicated on the left. We will mail the book first class and enclose a personalized gift card, too!

$19.95 plus $3.00 Postage and Handling for each book.
(Kansas residents add .625% sales tax)
Quantity discounts for groups and organizations
are available for 25 books and more.

Please print

Name ______________________________

Address ______________________________

City ____________________ State _____ Zip _______

Phone Bus. ________________ Home ____________

Please Mail To:

Name ______________________________

Address ______________________________

City ____________________ State _____ Zip _______

Phone Bus. ________________ Home ____________

Inscription on gift card ______________________

____

❑ Check Enclosed ❑ Money Order Enclosed
(Please make payable to Trust Publishing Company)

❑ MasterCard ❑ Visa ❑ American Express

Card # ____________________ Expiration Date ________

Cardholder's Signature ______________________

Mail to **Trust Publishing Company**
10308 Metcalf, Suite 257 • Overland Park, KS 66212

For faster service phone **Toll Free 1-800-835-0220 Extension 284**

Order Books for Gifts

STOP Probate NOW! The Only Living Trust Book You'll Ever Need is an excellent gift for your friends and loved ones. Ideal for birthdays, anniversaries, retirements and holidays, it makes a timely present that will be appreciated for years to come. The information in the book includes valuable answers for everyone who has serious questions about the high cost of Probate and the long court delays it involves. **Copy the order form** on this page or remove it where indicated on the left. We will mail the book first class and enclose a personalized gift card, too!

$19.95 plus $3.00 Postage and Handling for each book.
(Kansas residents add .625% sales tax)
Quantity discounts for groups and organizations
are available for 25 books and more.

Please print

Name ____________________

Address ____________________

City ____________________ State _____ Zip ________

Phone Bus. ____________________ Home ____________

Please Mail To:

Name ____________________

Address ____________________

City ____________________ State _____ Zip ________

Phone Bus. ____________________ Home ____________

Inscription on gift card ____________________

____

☐ Check Enclosed ☐ Money Order Enclosed
(Please make payable to Trust Publishing Company)

☐ MasterCard ☐ Visa ☐ American Express

Card # ____________________ Expiration Date ________

Cardholder's Signature ____________________

Mail to **Trust Publishing Company**
10308 Metcalf, Suite 257 • Overland Park, KS 66212

For faster service phone **Toll Free 1-800-835-0220 Extension 284**